MW01716674

To Rev. Pat!

DEVELOPING GOD'S LEADERS

Volume One

By

Rev. Dr. Robyn C. Edwards

An Avid Supporter!

Bright Light Publishers

Love You!

Robyn Edwards+

But the LORD said unto Samuel, Look not on his countenance, or on the height oj his stature; because l have refused him: for the LORD seeth not as man seeth; for man looketh on the outward appearance, but the LORD looketh on the heart.. 1 Samuel 16:7b

This Book Is Dedicated To:
Sharon Dunn, Pat West, Pastor Rebecca West, Elder Irene Robinson, Arlene Selman, Sheila Plummer, Vanessa Hazzard, Alanda Edwards, Joy Ryerson and Donna Turner.
I couldn't have made it this far without you.

Special Thanks To:
Beverley Locke, Rev. Amie Gardner, Rev. Rufus Pope, Craig Williams, Annyjah Hocutt, Ayo Majekodumni, Guerlyne Guercy and Sheila Paul.
For all of your hard work in making this effort possible.

Developing God's Leaders Volume 1
Copyright © 2013 by Robyn Edwards

ISBN 10: **0578128330**
ISBN 13: **978-0578128337**

Distributed by Bright Light Publishers, Inc.
P.O. Box 684, Pomona, NY 10970
For more information, please call 845-362-8900
Bright Light's Website: http:// www.brightlightpublishers.org

Unless otherwise indicated, all Scripture quotations are taken from The Holy Bible, King James Version ® (KJV) Copyright © King James Version, Cambridge, 1769. Used by permission. All rights reserved worldwide.

No part of this book may be reproduced or transmitted in any form or by any means, electronic, mechanical, including photocopying, without the written permission from the author.

All rights reserved.
Printed in the United States of America

Library of Congress Cataloging-in-Publication Data has been applied for.

Volume One: "Is There a Leader in the Midst?"

Table of Contents

But the LORD said unto Samuel, Look not on his countenance, or on the height of his stature; because I have refused him: for the LORD seeth not as man seeth; for man looketh on the outward appearance, but the LORD looketh on the heart.. 1 Samuel 16:7b

FORWARD

We have often heard the maxim 'a good man is hard to find.' Well, I take it just a little further and say that a good leader is hard to find. Leadership in the church is extremely challenging. The challenge is to reach out to people and direct them to the Lord Jesus Christ. But, the greatest challenge for most leaders is to follow—meaning follow God.

Rev. Dr. Robyn L. Edwards is one of the most exemplary leaders that I have ever known. She has given her life, time and resources to helping others find their way to the Lord Jesus Christ. She is also a great advocate of following God and following leadership.

In this book you will find the true definition of what it takes to care for the flock of Jesus Christ; to minister to ministers and to work with senior leaders. This book is a manual for bishops, pastors, ministers and laity. If we learn to follow, then we will be prepared to lead.

I believe the message of this book will enhance leadership relationship, teamwork connection and community bonding. Please take the time out to exhaust this book and reclaim godly shepherding.

Yours in the Master's Service,

Rev. Dr. J.E. McCullough

Senior Pastor, International Gathering at Beth Rapha

But the L*ORD said unto Samuel, Look not on his countenance, or on the height of his stature; because I have refused him: for the* L*ORD seeth not as man seeth; for man looketh on the outward appearance, but the* L*ORD looketh on the heart.. 1 Samuel 16:7b*

ACKNOWLEDGEMENTS

Thanks to those leaders that continue to groom me, and to those who gave me my start:

The Rev. Dr. Jacqueline E. McCullough: The indelible mark in my life, placed through working for and with you the last 20 years, being a member and leader in your flock of 12 years, and a mentee and best friend for an unrecorded space of time has been a privilege. Through our relationship, I have learned to love God fiercely and to uncompromisingly stand flat-footed in the face of all anti-Christ beliefs, seeing that the kingdom of our God advances.

Bishop Roderick Caesar: Your excellence, godly influence and extensive amount of ministerial training shaped my formative years in ministry and prepared me to be God's pastor and leader.

Pastor Beverly Caesar: My sister and best friend, our journey together began many years ago and nothing could replace the shared moments and memories. Your presence in my life has left me fully enriched and I would not have been the same without you.

Ever my spiritual family and friends, I will never cease to be grateful for the 40 years of life, growth and teaching that The Lord gifted us with.

Pastor Beverly Caesar Sherrod: You have been an essential part of my ministerial training and support system. The example you displayed has equipped me for my life's assignment today.

Dr. Michael Torres. My friend and Colleague of 15 years, I celebrate the affinity you have for The Word of God and your uncanny ability to teach it with unmatched wisdom and revelation. You have ignited in me the fervor to continue to excel in the acquisition of the knowledge of God in order to be a vessel fit for its proper disposition to God's people.

And finally, to my Lord and Savior Jesus Christ, without whom I could do nothing; all that I do, I do for Him. Unto Him be all the honor, praise and glory!

Developing God's Leaders

"Is There A Leader In The Midst?"

Preface

It is indeed a joyful pleasure, as well as a burden, to begin writing on the topic of leadership. Many people have written on this topic and that has made me very reluctant to do so. However, I have realized that the Lord wants me to add to the body of literature out there as well. He has placed in me a burden and a love for leaders that I cannot ignore, and together with the experience and insight that He has given me, I believe that now is the time for me to complete this task.

I have been in the Church of Jesus Christ all of my life, and subsequently have found that one of the things that the church is lacking today is good leadership. We are still very much missing the mark in this area. Yet in Scripture, there are countless examples that show how God used many kinds of people (imperfect and otherwise) to be His leaders.

It is my humble opinion that those of us who train leaders in the church have failed to share these biblical examples as much as we have shared our own personal experiences. As a result of this, we have a generation of people that are utterly deficient in the things of God.

If this pattern is allowed to continue, the Church will be in deep trouble. I believe God will trouble the hearts of the few who are willing to really live the full measure of Christianity; and all that comes with it (suffering included!). It is clear that God is disquieting us not just to live out biblical leadership, but also to write the vision, and make it plain so that he who peruses it may hasten to save his life from the rash of mediocrity that plagues our churches today, by which so many shall be cut off (see Hab 2:2)[i].

Often we use the statement that "we are not perfect people." We know that God does not use perfect people; if He did, He would not be able to find such a person. However, He did say in Matthew 5:48, "Be ye therefore perfect, even as your Father which is in heaven is perfect."

The word *"perfect"* in that scripture means "to be growing into complete maturity of godliness in mind and character, having reached the proper height of virtue and integrity" (see *The Amplified Bible*). It shows us that we must be striving for completeness as our heavenly Father is complete.

So for us, that means that we must put people in place as leaders. When we do this, we need to know who and what we are working with. To that end, the title of this book is *Developing God's Leaders.* The chapters in this book are designed to provide you with ways to cultivate and develop His elect selection – those He has called to lead His people. This book can be read in any order that you wish as each chapter was written to stand on its own. However, if you are training your leaders, it will be beneficial to read it in its entirety.

I encourage you to read this book, and pass it on to those who are called to be leaders; especially those who are serious about being a leader for God. These leaders are those who are determined to persevere despite any difficulties or adversity surrounding them, knowing that God is ultimately in charge.

This material is also for those who have corrupt, passive and aggressive leadership around them. Even more importantly, this work is for those who have no leadership around them at all. God is still raising leaders today and His standards have not changed.

Working with ministers both at Bethel Gospel Tabernacle in Jamaica, New York, and The International Gathering at Beth Rapha in Pomona, New York, has given me the opportunity to understand the makings and the "ins and outs" of ministry. It has also given me the chance to deal with ministers and leaders of all types. Without these experiences, I would not have been able to make any of these assessments successfully.

So there you have it - not in its entirety, but it is a start. Good leadership is important in God's kingdom. If we all finally get on one accord in the area of developing God's leaders, we can focus on the real assignment of the Church today – saving souls! We have become distracted with the things that do not really matter. While we are still trying to figure out which church the Lord wants us to join; we have forgotten about the souls that are waiting for the opportunity to get to know Jesus. Those souls will simply die and go to hell if we do not step in and help.

Consider if you are ready to take this journey with God. After reading this book, you will find that you are in good company and that you have not been forsaken! God bless you on your journey.

But the LORD said unto Samuel, Look not on his countenance, or on the height of his stature; because I have refused him: for the LORD seeth not as man seeth; for man looketh on the outward appearance, but the LORD looketh on the heart.. 1 Samuel 16:7b

Unit I: Identifying God's Leaders

But the LORD said unto Samuel, Look not on his countenance, or on the height of his stature; because I have refused him: for the LORD seeth not as man seeth; for man looketh on the outward appearance, but the LORD looketh on the heart.. 1 Samuel 16:7b

Unit I: Identifying God's Leaders

But the LORD said unto Samuel, Look not on his countenance, or on the height of his stature; because I have refused him: for the LORD seeth not as man seeth; for man looketh on the outward appearance, but the LORD looketh on the heart.. 1 Samuel 16:7b

-1-

Who Are God's Leaders?

Grace Temple Church was in mourning after their pastor, Martin Seymour, passed away suddenly of a heart attack.

"He wasn't even sick," many said as they looked at each other in bewilderment. "What are we going to do?"

Pastor Seymour was a young man of 50 years and appeared fairly healthy. The members of this growing church unexpectedly found themselves making funeral arrangements.

His wife Alma however, struggled with all the arrangements because Pastor Seymour did not leave any personal plans in place. "He didn't plan to die right now," she said sadly, "He planned to live to a ripe old age." "He was so healthy," she exclaimed over and over. "What happened?"

Little did she realize that the confusion was just beginning. Not only did Pastor Seymour neglect to put his personal business in order, but he also overlooked the small detail of grooming leaders to take over the ministry in his demise. He never made the time to groom anyone to be leaders in the church!

There were some individuals that joined the ministry that had already been ordained as ministers, but he never took the time to put them in place in any way that would make the congregation feel safe.

Many started to panic and criticize; the same people that loved Pastor Seymour so dearly were now very critical of his negligence. Many left the church while others stayed, grumbling and complaining about the situation they found themselves in.

Leaders: Crucial To God's Plan

God places leaders in the midst of His plan for ministry. They are crucial to the plan for building up His Church. Those who are leaders already have a responsibility to identify potential leaders. Leaders are placed in the midst of a church to help with the vision that God has for each ministry that He has called forth. Therefore, if you are to find them, we must first understand what leaders are.

> "One of the first things Jesus did in His public ministry was to identify and develop future leaders who would advance his kingdom and mission (Mark 1:16-20; John 1:35-51). Paul modeled this as well, investing in emerging leaders like Timothy and Titus, among others.
> How are we doing with this crucial aspect of leadership in the church today? Are we building for the next generation, or have we overlooked this crucial component of our mission?"[ii]

Investing in Leaders Today

In the Winter 2010 edition of *Leadership Journal Magazine*, a survey asked pastors to respond to this statement: "I am intentionally investing in leaders who will emerge over the next ten years."[iii]

Most of the pastors that were asked strongly believed they were doing just that—"67 percent strongly agreed and 26 percent somewhat agreed."[iv] This was basically stating 93 percent were convinced that they are investing in emerging leaders. They also affirmed that the Church has a responsibility to develop future leaders.

But when asked to evaluate how well the Church is accomplishing the task of leadership development, although most agreed, they were not nearly as enthusiastic. In response to the statement:

"The Church does a good job fostering and developing new leaders," this time only 26 percent strongly agreed and 52 percent somewhat agreed, a drop in overall agreement of 15 percent. In addition, a significant amount of disagreement started to appear with the statement—21 percent either "somewhat" or "strongly disagreed".

The survey concluded, "While pastors believe that the Church is a place where leaders need to be developed and they see themselves investing in this task, they generally recognize a real deficit in the church's effectiveness in accomplishing it. Although efforts are being made, pastors are not confident that the church is nurturing and growing new leaders adequately."

The Church is Failing

We have seen a multitude of examples that leadership is failing all over the place; from politics to sports and other high ranking officials. It is no wonder that this same disease is seeping into the Church's portals and pulpits. Our senses are being dulled by the constant corruption in this evil and wicked world. This prevailing widespread failure leaves us to believe that corruption in ministry is not quite so unacceptable.

Yet we are encouraged in the Scriptures not to be conformed to this world but to allow ourselves to be transformed through regularly renewing of the mind, with information from the Word of God (See Romans 12:1-2). This tells me that there is hope in this seemingly hopeless situation that our churches are facing today.

Definitions of Leadership

There are many differing definitions of leadership that are so appropriate for this missive. Some basic concepts of what leadership looks like include:

- *One who acts as a guiding force*
- *One who motivates people towards a certain purpose or goal*
- *One who draws people into a certain course of action through persuasion or example*
- *One who gives direction and structure to others' work and efforts*
- *One who advises and coordinates others' ideas*

- *One who leads others into a life of holiness by example*
- *One who holds the authority to lead others by instruction or correction*[v]

These definitions may appear to be broad, but each of these qualities is necessary so that the ultimate goal of gathering souls for the Kingdom can be met. One very important trait that leaders are missing today is the ability to duplicate themselves, and the commitment to develop and train such leaders. It is interesting to note that in business, there is always a plan in place to groom (train and mentor), so that the basic tools for good leadership are not lacking. Why then can't the same apply to the church of God? A great number of churches are bereft of such tools.

The Church has done a major disservice in the area of grooming leaders. We have taken shortcuts that have been proven to destroy the very foundation of what is expected where leaders are concerned. This is shown when one is selected primarily on one's talent and gifting (which does not aid in the sanctification process) over the development of their character. We are so impressed with a person's gift that we fail to assist in the area of character building. We prove that we do not love their souls when we do not help them grow spiritually.

This does not put the responsibility on us as individuals to make sure that a person is going to heaven. That is God's job! But it does place the responsibility on us to make available sound teaching and training in the Word of God in order to encourage successful character building.

1 Corinthians 3:6-7 states that one plants, another waters but God gives the increase. There is always something that God will do for us, but we have our part to play as well. He will never do our part. The world does not care about character because it does not believe that a person can really change. When the struggles of alcohol, drugs and other "coping" problems occur, the world is more inclined to eventually put you aside rather than give you what is necessary for freedom from such bondages. This is because only the Savior can deliver a person from the bondage of anger, depression, alcohol, drugs, sexual addiction and the like.

Romans 10:11says, "For the Scripture says, "Whoever believes on Him will not be put to shame" (NKJV). The word shame in this text means disgrace or to be confused.[1] It is our job as pastors and teachers to aim (position) each person in the direction where they will not be disgraced or confused. Romans 10:14 says, "How then shall they call upon Him in whom they have not believed? And how shall they believe in Him whom they have not heard? And how shall they hear without a preacher?" (NASB) Preachers are necessary to the purpose of God. They are the mouthpieces that God has set in place to spread His word.

Verse 15 states, "And how shall they preach, except they be sent?" Where are the sent ones that will be the mouthpieces for God? Verse 17 says, "Faith cometh by hearing, and hearing by the word of God." What are we preaching?

The word of God; by this and not our noble principles, thoughts and belief systems, is the means by

---

[1] Biblesoft's New Exhaustive Strong's Numbers and Concordance with Expanded Greek-Hebrew Dictionary. Copyright © 1994, 2003, 2006 Biblesoft, Inc. and International Bible [illegible]

which character is taught. Although, we as leaders have a great deal of "systems" under our belt, it is the word of God that convicts, confronts and displeases most people. Therefore, it should be used to bring change in people's lives! This is the standard that so many Pastors have thwarted because of their dire need of affirmation and acceptance from their peers, congregation members and politicians at all costs.

In ignorance, the church has adopted the world's way. This is mainly because we are unaware of what the Bible says regarding character flaws and struggles, and the church's leaders are not preaching and teaching The Word. Why? Simply put, it is because some leaders are not using the Word of God for their own personal lives. How then can they use it to help others? The answer is that they can't. They can only give to others what they know personally.

However, all is not lost or hopeless! The Bible is still available for use to fill the breaks, voids and holes that we, as the Body of Christ, have left opened.

Groom the Leaders!

It is vitally important that we get back to the job of grooming and making leaders and not just selecting them. This process of grooming takes work, and many of us do not want to invest the time and effort required.

After all, it is not easy taking the time to pour into people who may not necessarily agree that they need pouring into. Many times resistance appears because that person has already reached a point where they are not open to teaching and grooming. They already see their own potential and are not interested in anything that you want to pour in, especially if the process requires what they deem to be regression or "back peddling." There is a way to catch them ahead of time though. This can be done by assisting them in applying the necessary principles, while encouraging the humility needed to be recognized as God's leaders. We can also take hold of those who have stepped forward into leadership without the principles and pour godly principles into them. This course of action for those particular persons may be somewhat different than it would be for others, but it does not necessarily have to be hopeless.

God is Always Grooming Leaders behind the Scenes

Before we go any further, we need to understand that there is not a shortage of leadership. God is always grooming for Himself a people that will show forth His praises (1 Pet. 2:9) and move forth in His purpose. He always has a remnant (1 Kings 19:18) who will duplicate themselves, for that is what God's leaders do. How many churches have we seen where the pastor can no longer shepherd due to illness, death or a great "falling away", and there is no person evident to take over the ministry? In many cases, if it were not for God showing us what He was doing behind the scenes, we would not have any leaders in place for these regretful situations. Because God is so faithful, He will begin to move forward the one who should be in place; and in such cases this person is the one He, in His omniscience, was grooming for the task all along.

The Grooming of David

A wonderful example of how God grooms is displayed in the life of David. First Samuel 17 tells the story of the Philistines gathering together against Israel at Ephes-dammim. After Saul and his men pitched their camp near the valley of Elah to meet the battle, Goliath of Gath, a gigantic man whose height was six cubits and a span, defied the armies of Israel, and proposed to end all contests by a single combat. Saul, Israel's leader at this time, and his host were greatly distressed.

Yet David, having been sent by his father to provide provision for his brothers in the army, heard the challenge, and began to inquire into the circumstances. It was evident to him that while this was a reproach to Israel and their God, there was no man found to accept the challenge.

In verses 13-32, we find that David was brought before Saul, and proposed to undertake the combat. When Saul objected to his youth and inexperience, we see that David began to talk about the way he was prepared for such a task. He did not attend any great formal training, which sometimes can disqualify us for the obvious mission ahead.[vi]

It is God's assignment to place us in the position where He wants us, but it is our assignment to be in tune with God. This means discerning His choices for leadership and doing what is necessary to prepare that person for the transition. God does not really need us as pastors to do what He has to do. It takes humility on our part for us to agree with His plan so that we do not get in the way. A part of that humility may mean that we are busy grooming a person for their purpose.

In 1 Sam. 17:32-37, we hear David's response as he briefly states that he, the servant, and not the savior, will go and fight the giant. Saul told David that he did not believe that he was competent to fight against the Philistine because he was not mature enough to handle the task, since this giant had been a warrior from his youth. David's response was that his unusual resume gave him the necessary skills to perform this task. One of his unique accomplishments included the killing of wild animals that came upon him while he was serving in the field tending sheep. Saul then had to give David consent to fight the Philistines, even though he felt that

David was not necessarily the right choice. His futile attempt for David to use the armor and tools that he thought would work was not the plan of God for David, even though David out of respect tried them on. Saul could have laughed at David and sent him on his way thereby putting Israel in danger. As pastors, we have to know what God is saying for each potential leader and know when not to cross His boundaries. Our preparation is miniscule in comparison to God's preparation, but God will not do our part. We have to recognize these leaders and put them in place.

Recognizing Leaders

Sometimes we are looking for leaders but are not recognizing the ones that God has placed in our midst. Perhaps we are looking for those that are already showing signs of doing what they do well as opposed to looking at those who show signs of loving God and wanting to please Him. God will place in these people a love for souls and a love for His plans. Once a person is moving in the direction of strong spiritual growth, you have a potential leader in your midst. This person can be groomed and trained to do what is needed; and is grounded in the ministry enough to begin being an asset to the ministry.

In I Kings 19:14-18, Elijah complained. He had passionately served the LORD, but bemoaned the people of Israel for breaking their covenant with God, tearing down His altars, and killing every one of His prophets. He felt that he was the only one left to do God's will. But listen to God's response to him. God said He had preserved for Himself "seven thousand others in Israel who have never bowed to Baal or kissed him" (NLT). This tells me that not only does God have a remnant, but that He preserves them for His purpose! Somewhere there was an Elisha being prepared to come onto the scene; and in God's perfect timing, that person came forth.

We simply need to understand God's way of choosing. This was a key factor in David's story (I Sam. 16:5-12) and it was also a key factor in Elisha's story. God does the selecting and He always has someone that He is grooming for His purpose. Often it is one that has not bowed their heads to their own agendas, nor given in to the world's standard, and is somewhere in the process waiting to be called forth to be used of the Lord.

Be obedient to what God says, and anoint the one He is grooming!

Hindrances to proper grooming: The Perils of Pride

Grooming someone for leadership may not be easy because pride can take over. We sometimes can feel insecure, inadequate, rejected and "washed up". These strong feelings of self-pity (otherwise known as pride) are sure to stop any leader from choosing another to assist in some way. In order to deter this from happening, we must obey the wooing of the Holy Spirit to handle God's ministry God's way. If we choose to obey our prideful flesh, then the enemy will use these lies to ultimately bring forth our own demise in some way.

A hardworking young man working in the ministry selling CDs and DVDs at the ministry table may think he will be taking over that particular area of ministry. However, he may not know that working with the senseless supervisor in the same department will prepare him to work with a senseless, "fire breathing" associate pastor in the church where the Lord will be placing him.

We do not always know what the future holds, and we do not always know why the Lord is grooming us in a particular area. We just have to flow with Him and choose to find ourselves in His will, and not in the secret desires of our deceiving hearts. I worked for many years as a manager of a Christian bookstore, not realizing that I was being prepared to assist in pastoring a church one day. It may not always look as if things are lined up properly, but do not try to figure God out!

What Should the Proper Response Be?

If you believe that you are being groomed by God to lead, you may not see the whole picture. I suggest you not try to step into anything without letting the Lord do His work. Most times, you may appear to be unqualified for the position for which The Lord is preparing you, but He will do what is necessary through your suffering and tribulation to prepare you for the assignments at hand. 1 Kings 19:19-20 is a wonderful example of what happens when a person is set aside for grooming.

Verse 19 says, Elijah departed and found Elisha, who was "plowing with twelve yoke of oxen before him". This suggests that Elisha was busy serving. It is important that we be found serving and not waiting to be noticed. Often, we are serving and waiting for our "moment," or serving and complaining to God about what we should be doing in ministry. God is always preparing us when we are serving.

Sometimes we are discouraged if we believe that the present leader does not "see us". The scripture does not specifically say that Elijah knew anything about Elisha, but that it was the Lord Himself who revealed that Elisha should be put in place and instructed Elijah (the leader at this point) to begin to groom him. It was during this time that Elijah passed by him, and cast his mantle upon him indicating that he was beginning his grooming process with Elisha. God never misses opportunities; we simply frustrate ourselves trying to figure out what God is working out. He is deliberate and precise in all His doings.

Have An Eye for Leaders

Above all things, you must first know what you are looking for, because a leader can be spotted in a number of places. You will know them because they are those whom God has chosen to rule, guide and inspire others; God will point them out to you. If you bear that in mind, you will be able to find leaders anywhere, even in preschool settings. Initially these youngsters may have had leaders in their homes, and have naturally picked up the art of leadership. Observe them in their dealings with their peers and you will soon see that they were born to inspire others.

Start the Process Early

Get started training your leaders early in their productive years. The qualities that are necessary for good leadership can be cultivated even during the elementary school years. You must be very careful, for children are very impressionable and can pick up negative traits as well as positive ones. This being the case, you must be deliberate in your doings and watch the examples set before them. While teaching precepts are important, examples teach as well. This does not mean you have to be the one to execute the training, it may just mean you need to oversee that it is being done.

If leadership skills are nurtured at a young age, some of the challenges that parents face with their children like "following the crowd", can be thwarted even before it begins. Children love to be accepted as part of a group. In junior high school, they are so desperate to be a part of a group that they will do anything to "fit in". In high school, there is more of a desire to be accepted, yet with a level of independence. Trends begin to surface from those who want to stand out and be noticed, to those who inwardly are looking to lead others to follow their trend. This is where the characteristics of leadership begin to surface and take shape.

When David was chosen by God, it was not his outward appearance that qualified him in God's eyes. Rather, he was distinguished by his heart, spirit and genuine love for God. When the time came for Samuel to anoint one of Jesse's sons, he almost selected the person that would not satisfy God! You have to be careful about the choices you make that mistakenly overlook and underestimate whom God has chosen. Samuel could have failed in his frailty by making a fleshly choice. But because he actually did love, know and hear God; he was able to make God's choice instead. Samuel was able to hear God to make known, display, declare, anoint, and appoint God's elect. In selecting and grooming the next leader, leaders should keep in mind that God is looking at the candidate's heart, while man is looking at his appearance. This fact must be important to today's leader when preparing and passing the baton to tomorrow's leader.

The Conclusion of the Matter

God has set His leaders in our midst and it is our job to recognize them and begin preparing them for work in the ministry. This may mean discerning where to place them as well; and discernment takes relationship on our part with God so that we are not a hindrance to the cause. Some leaders will be groomed to work alongside us and others will be groomed to eventually leave us for another great assignment. It is our job to agree with God so that we will unselfishly groom them for the work to which the Lord has called them, for whether it is with us or in another part of the vineyard, it is still The Lord's work.

But the LORD said unto Samuel, Look not on his countenance, or on the height of his stature; because I have refused him: for the LORD seeth not as man seeth; for man looketh on the outward appearance, but the LORD looketh on the heart.. 1 Samuel 16:7b

Chapter Reflections

To Potential Leaders:

1. Are you a leader that God has chosen?
2. Have you been effectively groomed?
3. If you have not been groomed effectively, what are the areas that you need assistance with?

Plan of Action:

Begin to pray and (perhaps) fast, asking God to show you where you should be working in your church at this particular time. Plant yourself in these areas and wait for your next set of instructions while God is fulfilling His plan.

To Pastors:

1. What type of leaders do you see in your midst?
2. Have you begun the grooming of potential leaders and if so, can you identify any areas where you may have **watered** down your grooming?

Plan of Action:

Begin to pray, and (perhaps) fast, asking God to show you who He may be identifying in your midst. In order to discern more clearly, The Lord may be requiring you to make changes in your personal life.

Make a commitment to begin grooming and stay accountable with someone so that you do not slack up in your responsibility to God due to busyness or discouragement.

-2-

Where Do You Find God's Leaders?

In the passing of her husband, Pastor Seymour's wife Alma began to pray. She began to feel a "leading of the Lord" to identify those that would help continue the legacy that her husband left behind. She would need to possibly find a bishop who could perhaps ordain anyone who needed credentials and others that needed to be put in place to assist in carrying the load.

Some of the people she felt that God identified were obvious to her: there was Brother and Sister Trumbull, great financial supporters and equally supportive of the vision. Then there was Ervin the choir director, a great motivator (for the choir members), who could really be helpful in assisting to shepherd the flock. Additionally there was Justice Turner, or "Turner" as he was known, who had a burden for the organizational aspect of the church. He assisted Pastor Seymour in many of his administrative endeavors and while he was a little passive in handling things, he was familiar with the way things should be run. Finally there was Sheila and Larry Dray, who were friends of the ministry and were always willing to give Pastor Seymour suggestions on how to run a successful ministry.

There was one problem with Sis. Alma's suggestions though. Some of these people were not regular members in the church. Although Brother and Sister Trumbull were great supporters, they traveled a great deal to their home in Florida. While they did support the ministry financially, they came sporadically and often stayed away six months out of the year in their Florida home. They were never really committed to the ministry even though they offered financial and emotional support.

Ervin, the choir director, was a great motivator for the choir members, but was also one of six choir directors from Fifth Avenue Baptist Church, a prominent church up the street. Ervin was like a son to Alma and Martin Seymour but they often encouraged him in his endeavors at Fifth Avenue Baptist Church.

Justice Turner, or "Turner" was only 20 years old, and many of his family members wanted him to go away to college in another state. Justice would give anything to work in the ministry, but his family wanted "more" for him.

Finally, Sheila and Larry Dray were not regular members in any church. They could not commit themselves to any ministry simply because whenever they did so they were often offended. This was a sign that they were spiritual babes and not "meat eaters" (Heb 5:12-14). Since they were churchgoers and had been a part of so many churches they used their criticism as wisdom for Pastor Martin and his wife Alma, who didn't seem to know the difference.

You do not want just any leader; you want the leader that God has placed in your midst. God is not negligent;

He is always grooming leaders even before we recognize them. So where do we find God's leaders?

God's Leaders Can Be Found Planted in the House of the Lord

How many pastors are in search of good leaders and are suffering from the lack of them? One of the main reasons for this is they find themselves looking beyond the portals of their own front doors. It is quite common for pastors to look outside of their own congregations for leaders when the best candidates are the ones that are planted in their own churches. Consider if you will, the following scripture:

> *Those that be planted in the house of the Lord shall flourish in the courts of our God. They shall still bring forth fruit in old age; they shall be fat and flourishing; To shew that the Lord is upright: he is my rock, and there is no unrighteousness in him. Psalm 92:13*

The image is that of a plant. "That is, the beauty, the erectness, the stateliness, the growth of the palm tree - all this is an emblem of the condition, the prosperity, the happiness of a righteous man." Barnes Notes compares the wicked to the righteous; it tells us that the wicked "shall be cut down" and that, the righteous will flourish. The comparison of the righteous man to a flourishing, majestic, green, and beautiful tree is what you need to look for when scouting out God's leaders.[2] This suggests that if a person is firmly planted in the Church, they will flourish; Plants do not grow indoors by themselves, they need nurturing. Plants that grow outside have the elements of nature to see to its' growth. Christians also need nurturing like plants do, (that is to be watered, cultivated and watched) to grow in the house of God.

A person who is planted in the house of the Lord is a person who is successfully settled in a church home which the Lord has chosen for them. There are three ways that constitute whether or not God has chosen a particular church home for an individual. One way, is to be physically born there or brought there by their parents at an early age.

---

[2] Barnes' Notes, Electronic Database Copyright © 1997, 2003 by Biblesoft, Inc. All rights reserved.

Another way is to be spiritually birthed there (meaning the place where they accepted the Lord Jesus Christ as their personal Savior). It should be noted that because a person accepts Jesus in a certain church does not mean that particular place has to be their church home. But they must plant themselves in a Bible-believing church as soon as they accept the Lord, so that they can begin to mature in their new walk.

The final way that constitutes whether or not God has chosen a particular church home for an individual is when the Lord (with confirmation) prompts them to join a particular assembly. This is the way that is most abused by those in the Church today. How many times have we heard the statements, "The Lord is moving me to another church," or "The Lord told me to go to another church"? These statements are often made out of offense, disappointment and disillusionment. It is easy to go to another church, but it is not easy to deal with the things that cause you to be unhappy in your present church. The offense that a person may be carrying will not be forgotten, simply by moving from church to church. It is so crucial when you leave a church that your decision is a "God decision" and not a decision coming from damaged emotions or offense of some sort. Today, it is unusual to find many who will stay in one particular church for a long period of time. The views of many Christians today clearly state, "What can you do for me?"

A newly appointed pastor of a local assembly suffered in this area of keeping members planted for three years. After the departure of several people within the first two to three months of attending, he overextended the church budget by adopting the practice of having concerts once a month featuring leading gospel artists and bringing in well-known conference speakers, all in an attempt to "hold on" to the members that would not plant themselves. The fickle crowds that flocked to the little church eventually left him for a ministry with another agenda of interest because they never knew what it was to really be planted in a church.

What Does It Mean To Be Planted in the House of the Lord?

It means to go to church and live your life there. Please do not mistake what I am saying. This does not mean that you are actually living in the church building 24 hours, seven days a week (although many find themselves there just that often). It means that you must settle yourself (spirit, soul and body) there, for your church is your spiritual home base. It is where you receive spiritual nurturing, and training and the "watching of your soul". It is where we learn what loving and knowing God is all about. It is the job of a good shepherd or pastor to provide opportunities whereby we can grow. Singing in the choir, baking for picnics and dinners, attending classes and encouraging other members, are some of the ways that we "forsake not the assembling of ourselves together" (Heb. 10:25). It is also the place where we as iron sharpen others who are iron as well (Pr. 27:17). Then, we go to our homes and jobs and live out what we have been taught in the house of the Lord. However, many of us miss out on these benefits because we do not believe that it "takes all that."

So then, what does flourishing look like? Having been planted in the house, an individual will grow, send out their branches and produce fruit there.[vii] If a person is firmly planted in the Church and the things of God, their fruit will be evident. These are perfect candidates for ministry – and future leadership.

One who is not planted in a church home and has a tendency to move around searching for another church home can be a detriment to the ministry. A person who has been planted cannot survive unless they continue to be planted. If you have a member that comes to your church from another ministry and has had longevity with the other ministry, it is not likely that they will do a great deal of moving because they are used to being planted. Therefore, it is important that you find out why a person is leaving their ministry or church home. They should have a good reason unless there was some form of offense. This can be dealt with sometimes quickly or over time with a little help. If each church dealt with those who move from church to church, Christians would be forced to deal with the problems they are trying so hard to avoid.

A noted gospel singer found herself disillusioned by a few things that her pastor stated from the pulpit. Although she was a gifted singer, she had no spiritual depth. Instead of getting clarity, she became offended and stopped attending her church. She began to attend other churches, but was not treated, in her opinion, the way a person of her gifting and talent should be treated, so she never joined any other ministry. This singer eventually stopped going to church altogether, and became carnal. Her melodious and anointed voice soon lost its powerful effect on those who sought after her. She attempted to study the Word on her own, but most times, because of her lack of discipline in studying the Scriptures, she generally took the Scriptures out of context. This was something most of her "fans" noticed right away. Eventually, her ministry no longer had the effect on those it was originally intended to minister to.

Jesus' Commentary on Being Planted.

In Chapter 15 of the Gospel of Matthew, we see Jesus speaking to the Pharisees about their traditions. He told them that their practices and habits violated the direct commandments of God. This can also be true for so many hurting individuals. How they handle their pain and offense can breach the very principles of the Word of God. We are often far more attached to customs, traditions and "family commandments" than Biblical principles. Beware of those that have a tendency to explain away the Word of God. It may seem too strict for them, and perhaps they may even say that it is too spiritual as well. They can be very skillful not to attack it directly, "but they will explain it and dilute it so as to make it mean nothing."[3] Notice how Jesus instructs His disciples to respond:

> *"But he answered and said, Every plant, which my heavenly Father hath not planted, shall be rooted up. 14 Let them alone: they be blind leaders of the blind. And if the blind lead the blind, both shall fall into the ditch." (Matt 15:13-14)*

When Jesus refers to "plant" here, he is referring to doctrine or our belief systems. These will not stand. When our Lord Jesus said, "Let them alone," He was letting us know to not be troubled at their rage, and

---

[3] Barnes' Notes, Electronic Database. Copyright (c) 1997 by Biblesoft

neither allow it to make us anxious. This result is to be expected. These church hoppers are greatly attached to their ways of handling things, and we are not to wonder why they are resentful, but instead we should address their error and make the necessary attempts to refute them. In His explanation, Jesus was in fact teaching His disciples that opposition was to be expected.[4]

If we fail to correct wrong information and address offenses in people, they will lead others into their crooked doctrines. When a person comes into your congregation with erroneous doctrines and heresies and is not corrected, you will be doomed to correct it on a larger scale once that person affects those around them. In 1 Corinthians 5:6-7, the Apostle Paul says, "a little leaven leaveneth the whole lump." Therefore, we have a mandate to "purge out" the old leaven.

---

[4] ibid

Addressing the Unstable Soul

Most people that move from church to church, or ministry to ministry within the church, show strong signs of instability. James 1:8 states, "A double minded man is unstable in all his ways." Don't deceive yourself into thinking that the instability is isolated to one area in particular in their lives. The Scripture clearly says "all their ways."

More times than not, there are unresolved situations that cause these unstable persons to have little or no commitment. Unless you assist them with these unresolved areas, they will eventually keep moving until they end up in a state of inactivity. They may perhaps be searching for an unrealistic situation where they can control the environment around them so that they do not experience the hurt that may have occurred in the past. Sometimes they are not even aware that they are doing this; but it is important that you are aware of it so that you do not experience any unnecessary surprises.

I once met with a young lady who was excited about joining our church and was ready to get busy at being such a help to us with what she called "expertise in the field of helping the pastors to build their church". She said she had helped several pastors and went down the list of her resume of churches that she assisted and was eager to begin with us. When I asked why she never stayed at these churches, the truth began to manifest itself in her explanations. She never wanted to sit down and be fed by these churches. "I just want to help" she claimed. But you cannot be a leader in a church and not submit yourself to receive ministry from the church. This was a sure sign of a lack of trust on her part. This does not mean that you won't be able to be fed from anywhere else; it just means that if you work for a restaurant and yet you find that you do not eat at that restaurant; there is probably a "strong" reason for this decision. Perhaps you do not trust the food because you have inside information. The same could be the case for this young lady – she had inside information about the church she had been attending. The real reasons as to why she left needs to be dealt with before considering a move to another church. This young lady would stay in a state of offense because of what she saw and experienced behind the scenes. She would then move to the next church hoping to find a more perfect situation, only to add more offense to her already offended stance due to her unrealistic expectations.

Be careful not to pull leaders from other churches. It can be complicated and detrimental to both churches involved. You may not be familiar with some of their problems and you may be taking on more than you can handle in doing so. Additionally, the other pastor may become offended and then you may also start reaping similar situations in your congregation. You do not want anyone that was a constant source of problems in their former church to join your ministry, thinking they will give you service any different from what they have already rendered to their former leader. If they have problems respecting the authority at one church, chances are you can look forward to the same disrespect to your authority as well. Learn to look deeper into the situation and assist that person in working out their differences with their former leaders. Romans 12:18 says, "If it be possible, as much as lieth in you, live peaceably with all men." We should encourage people to work toward a peaceable solution in order to move forward. If unresolved anger is held, it will only lead to evil doings (Ps. 37:8, Eph 4:26).

Why Do People Leave Churches?

As stated earlier, there can be several reasons why a person will leave their former church. However, one reason that is prominently used is "the Lord has instructed me to do so." Just bear in mind if the Lord is speaking to the individual, always remember that "it is the same God who works all in all" (1 Cor. 12:6-7, NKJV). We have the freedom in knowing that God will not just speak to one person, but can and will speak to all the parties involved in some way, form or fashion. This means that God will speak to not only the church where the individual is leaving, but the church that is receiving the individual as well.

There are several occasions where a pastor has to send a person back to a fellowship, where they cunningly believe they have been released. If we probe a little deeper, we will find that there is some unresolved offense that is under the "peace" that these people claim to have. It is our job as pastors (who are assigned to guard the flocks), to pull the offense to the surface and encourage people to deal with the resentment that is perhaps building up in those members who are running from their former church homes. It may not happen overnight, but the process is necessary for spiritual growth and alignment.

Many people have their reasons for leaving their churches, but their reasoning should not usurp the authority of Scripture. These people should be informed that they are in error and that they should seek the appropriate biblical response to their offenses. In some cases, biblical counseling will be necessary.

God's Leaders will Flourish

Our scripture in Psalm 92, verse 14 informs us, that the planted ones "shall still bring forth fruit in old age; they shall be fat and flourishing." This gives us a picture of what to expect long after the planted ones become of full age. They are always producing and they do not retire. They do not ever stop serving or giving to the Body of Christ in some way. However, there may be a redefining of how they operate during the different seasons or stages in their lives. Even if you no longer have the physical strength due to age or sickness, true leaders can continue to be useful by encouraging and praying for others; perhaps via a prayer line. These people are often found displaying the faithfulness and stability of God (vs. 15) in their lives. Such persons are testimonies to the promises of God and the truth of His Word.[viii] They do not retire, but redefine themselves as God gives direction. They may not jump up and down in the youth choir after a time, but may be very capable of giving advice to a discouraged individual. In addition, they may also be well suited in preparing curriculum for specific classes in the Sunday School Department.

The Conclusion of the Matter.

Where can you find God's leader? They can be found planted in the house of the Lord (in His church) flourishing and going through different seasons of their lives, and ultimately, enduring hardship as a good soldier (2 Tim. 2:3). Flourishing, no matter what the season in their lives, is evident of one who is planted.

But the LORD said unto Samuel, Look not on his countenance, or on the height of his stature; because I have refused him: for the LORD seeth not as man seeth; for man looketh on the outward appearance, but the LORD looketh on the heart.. 1 Samuel 16:7b

Chapter Reflections

To Potential Leaders:

1. Are you one who has moved from church to church? Identify the trust problems that you are struggling with and state where it first began.
2. Have you been in more than one church over the past three to five years? What were some of the reasons for your moves?
3. Are you blaming others for the decisions you made to leave those churches? What would you say you have done to add to the problem?

Plan of Action:

To begin moving out of the bondage of a lack of trust, deepen your relationship with the Lord. Once you really start trusting God, you will trust His decisions on who should lead you, and where you should be planted. God's ways are not like our ways. Change needs to take place within you and your relationship with the Lord. Once this happens, you will be able to fully agree with God (not be compliant), and thus plant yourself successfully where the Lord wants you to be.

To Pastors:

1. How many of your leaders are "churchgoers", and how many are "planted" ones?
2. Have you identified those who are God's choice for leaders in your congregation?
3. Can you identify those that are not stable in your midst? What are some of the unstable ways that you have observed?
4. Does your church have a revolving door? If so, what do you believe to be some of the causes?

Plan of Action:

Pray and ask God to show you those who are stable, as well as those who are not, so that you can begin helping potential leaders specifically where they are. Be open to what He will reveal and the way He chooses to reveal it. He may use a trusted person or one that is stable to share their views with you.

But the LORD said unto Samuel, Look not on his countenance, or on the height oj his stature; because I have refused him: for the LORD seeth not as man seeth; for man looketh on the outward appearance, but the LORD looketh on the heart.. 1 Samuel 16:7b

-3-

How to Recognize Potential Leaders

Grace Temple Church was now in the place where they would begin to identify the leaders that would help take the ministry to the next level. Sister Alma went to Pastor Steve Stiff, pastor of Fifth Avenue Baptist Church. He seemed to know what he was doing; his church was thriving with leaders and full of growing souls. She sat down and asked him all of her questions, hoping he would have answers for each of them.

He encouraged her to understand that God had leaders planted in Grace Temple, and she would need to use her discernment to begin to recognize them. He began to walk her through some of the biblical ways to recognize a planted person (potential leader), who was ready to bloom.

Recognizing potential leaders

Now that you know the definition of a leader, and where to locate them, you need to know if there are any in your midst. God is constantly developing His leaders, but how do you recognize them?

Since you are not able to see the heart, there are some ways that you can be in agreement with God. Through spiritual discernment and observation, you can begin to notice them. In every area of the church, there are budding leaders waiting to blossom and bloom.

Scan the audience of your congregation and take a general look. There are some whose leadership capabilities are more visible than others. But what in particular are we seeking? Is it only for one who has attained certain skills?

First, you must look for true Christians. I know this may sound a little silly, but sometimes pastors can compromise in this area. We discussed in Chapter 1 how Samuel almost made a choice outside of God's will by looking at the outward presentation of Jesse's sons. He didn't do so because he had an intimate relationship with God. So when we are looking for leader, we have to not look at what they present to us, we have to know if they have a relationship with God! Some cases will not be as evident as other cases. For instance, we might choose someone who is religious or one that does not mind using their leadership ability in the church; but that has no real relationship with God. This can be dangerous because their ethics would differ greatly from those of the household of faith

A friend of mine who is a pastor once hired a young lady who was very good with young people. This young lady worked as a schoolteacher during the day and at an afterschool program for troubled youth twice weekly. The progress she showed with young people was tremendous in the eyes of the pastor, so he offered this young lady a salaried position in the church as a youth minister.

It did not take long before the efforts of this young lady went sour after making decisions for the young people's ministry that were not in keeping with biblical views. Going to popular, compromising R-rated movies and late night parties that conflicted with the church's activities were among the several outings in which this youth leader saw "nothing wrong." The young woman's leadership greatly compromised the views of the house and many of the young people adopted her phrase, saying that there was "nothing wrong" with the worldly views of their peers that were not even Christians. Eventually these young people found themselves involved in everything but the things of God. There were a few that had a hunger for God and found themselves being taunted by the majority of those whose stance was that "it didn't take all that."

After losing several young people to worldly things that were more important to them than the things of God, this pastor had to lovingly dismiss this person from her position before any more damage was done. While he spoke the truth in love, this young lady could not handle the disappointment. She was not spiritually mature enough to understand the pastor's view; she became offended, causing her and her family to eventually leave the church, along with several young people who had grown attached to her.

Good Christians Make Good Leaders

Good Christians are not perfect Christians. Matthew 16:24 says, "Then said Jesus unto his disciples, if any man will come after me, let him deny himself, and take up his cross, and follow me." By denying Himself, Jesus is letting each of us know the character of those who want to follow Him. Denying is the act of giving up one's desires and plans for themselves and taking on God's desires and plans for one's life. Embracing the Cross involves the giving up of our agendas and motives for His ultimate plan.

To take up one's cross, is to embrace the struggles that come with the walk which God has assigned, and bear those troubles and difficulties we may meet walking the Christian road. When Jesus took up His Cross, He embraced the will of the Father with a "nevertheless" attitude (Luke 22:42).

The Scripture further tells us, "For whosoever will save his life shall lose it: and whosoever will lose his life for my sake shall find it" (Matthew 16:25). Here we understand that we have but one life and there are two roads to take. We can take a road that is selfish - saving, scraping and fighting for what we want for that life. Or we can give our desires over to God and receive the life that God has already mapped out for us.

This type of lifestyle is mandatory for Christians—not just Christian leaders, but anyone that is willing to be a follower of Christ. While many claim to be Christians, not many are willing to embrace their struggles and lose their lives for God.

What does it mean to be a good Christian? It means doing what the Word says. It is having a desire to do what is right.

Every church has those members that are able to maintain a proper walk without a great deal of maintenance. It is this person that should be singled out and sought after for leadership grooming. If they are able to get information from the weekly sermons, they are able to take feeding. If they are able to "hold the Word" without losing it (Matt. 13:8), it is likely that they will become doers of the Word (James 1:22).

There are so many Christians that miss the message coming forth every week because they do not have the discipline to hold the Word. These people will never make good leaders. If they do not hold the Word now, they will not hold it later because that person's soul is not deeply convinced of its guilt and depravity. The fallow ground of their sinful hearts is not properly plowed up, nor is the slab of rock (stony or hard heart) broken that blocks them from their change. Therefore, when unexpected persecution comes, they soon stumble and seek some excuse to abandon both the doctrine and even the very followers of Christ. This Christian, having not felt his own sore, and the plague of his heart, he has not properly discovered that this salvation is the only remedy for his soul. As a result, he has no motive in his heart strong enough to counteract the outward scandal of the Cross; so he endures only for the time in which there are no difficulties to encounter.[ix]

Paul said in his epistle to the Corinthian church that these people will be carnal in their doings. We have a responsibility to water that seed of the Gospel that has been first planted in the people of God. We water it by the preachings, teachings and exhortations, but only God can give the increase. It is He who will convince each of us of our "guilt and depravity."[x]

If you want good leaders, begin to make disciples! They will become people who will have a love for God, and can receive the Word and do the Word. 1 John 2:4-5 says, "He who says, 'I know Him,' and does not keep His commandments, is a liar, and the truth is not in him. But whoever keeps His word, truly the love of God is perfected in him. By this we know that we are in Him" (NKJV*)*. Spend time pouring into the new converts and make them into disciples. Get a hold of them while they are pure and have a desire to get to know God. Teach them how to run after God and make Him their choice.

Some Christians will show leadership capability and others may need a little guidance and training. Develop the people so that they can understand what being a leader is. Have leadership seminars and training classes so that they can assist in the care of the flock. Make every Christian their brother's keeper by teaching them to see problems and address them.

If every Christian went around helping other Christians, the pastor would have less work. There was a time when I would get so angry when I would hear the saints gossip. It would upset me so that I would never say anything to the person, but instead would sometimes tell the pastor because of the good relationship we had. But I found out that telling the pastor and not allowing him to address the situation would never change things. At that point, it became evident that what I was doing was gossiping also because it only let the pastor know things that he could not address without compromising what seemed to be "my integrity".

The Lord helped me understand that my reluctance to allowing the pastor to address that person meant that I was not open to correcting them either. If I really believed that gossip was not right, I wouldn't find myself gossiping to the pastor about the members. I knew I had to change. I eventually realized that one did not have to be a pastor to correct gossiping people. I did what I needed to do humbly and in love, because I knew that I too had been gossiping. Sure, they did not like it and they made comments, and some even justified their behavior. But I stood my ground and those who really wanted to change, repented and began to grow. Still, others just went undercover not allowing me to hear the gossip. After some time, it became evident what I was going to say if anyone came to me, and while people heard the Word and claimed to believe it, they did not do the Word (James 1:22) and therefore found themselves staying away from me.

After a while, word started getting out that I was one that would correct certain behaviors. I felt that if people knew the seriousness of sin, they would let it go. I always gave people the benefit of the doubt, thinking surely if they knew it was wrong they would not do it. I began to search the Scriptures so that I would have an explanation for my "theories." I would lovingly share what the Word said and this is what began the road of leadership for me. When people heard what I was doing, people that wanted more of God would flock around me and others would mark me as an enemy. Then, of course, you had those that did not want to change.

I became blackballed by the underground subculture of that church — yes, the underground - every church has one. These people can befriend those who are just like them causing these people to multiply. The problem is those people do not mind duplicating themselves. We as Christians should have the same zeal of duplicating ourselves, developing a stronger culture against those who don't truly want God. Many times the "wicked" people in the church are allowed to run rampant through flock, splitting up and dividing congregations. Most times all that is needed is a few good Christians that will speak up. These same Christians who do not mind standing up to gossipers or who will not tolerate gossip can make excellent leaders.

Fruitful People Make Good Leaders

We have stated that those that are planted flourish and are fruitful. This means that those that are fruitful make great leaders. Matthew 13:23 says that the one that receives the Word of God and understands it is like one that received seed into the good ground;

this person will bear fruit, not just a little fruit but some a "hundredfold, some sixty, some thirty."

Are there fruitful people in your ministry? These people are those who at some point and time get active in ministry and become an asset to those areas of ministry. These individuals must show the fruit of the Spirit – beware of those who exhibit the gifts of the Spirit without the fruit. We must encourage and exhort God's people to bear fruit, for in Jesus' parable of the barren fig tree (Luke 13:6-9), except a tree brings forth fruit, "it will be cut down."[xi]

I know that many have said to themselves, "Is not the ground naturally bad in every heart?" Adam Clarke in his *Commentary* tells us, "Undoubtedly." He further states,

> *"And can any but God make it good? None. But it is your business, when you hear of the justice and mercy of God, to implore him to work in you that which is pleasing in his sight. No man shall be condemned because he did not change his own heart, but because he did not cry to God to change it, who gave him his Holy Spirit for this very*

> *purpose, and which he, by his worldly-mindedness and impiety, quenched. Whoso hath ears to hear let him hear: and may the Lord save the reader from an impenitent and unfruitful heart!"*[xii]

The dresser of the vineyard engages to do his part, which should encourage ministers to do theirs (Luke 13:6-9). When Jesus states that, "he will dig about the tree and will dung it," it tells us that God's hand is very much involved in the fruit-bearing process. "Unfruitful Christians must be awakened by the terrors of the law, which break up the fallow ground, and then encouraged by the promises of the gospel, which are warming and fattening, as manure to the tree. Both methods must be tried; the one prepares for the other".[xiii]

When God is actively involved in pruning, digging and dunging His people, these people can become prime candidates for leadership in the Church. How they respond to the hand of God in this area is key. Scripture tells us that we must be clothed in humility, because God resists the proud. We, therefore, are to humble ourselves under the mighty hand of God (1

Peter 5:5-7). Those who do are prime candidates for exaltation from the Lord.

Good Followers Make Good Leaders

Good Christians make excellent followers, however it is possible to have Christians that are not good followers. Many times it may be a result of a terrible childhood that stops a person from respecting and revering leadership. These people have good intentions, but they find it hard to trust leaders based on what they went through with their "first leaders"—their parents. A young man can find it very hard to follow a male Pastor if he is angry at his own father for not being present. A young female may do the same. This is not always definite, but many times it can be a part of the problem. While some may be hungry for the affirmation of male leadership, still others will blatantly shy away. Their trust level has to be built and their broken hearts mended. This, however, cannot take place without a person first learning to trust God. It is a genuine relationship with the Lord that will begin to bud with signs of trust for others.

If you find that you have people who have trouble following leadership, don't be so quick to throw them away. Try pouring in the healing salve and watch what the Lord will do. This process takes work and sometimes endless selfless endeavors to see that the person stays on track. It will definitely take some time, but be patient and you will begin to see the results of a God that can heal.

People Who Are Willing To Help Others Make Good Leaders

As stated earlier, Christian character is not just for the Christian leader but for all Christians, no one is exempted. I know so many Christians who are very spiritual and yet they do not seek to help others in their walk unless invited to do so. This makes us limited. It means that we would be willing to help only those that accept us or specifically ask for help, rather than helping those that we see struggling. The struggling Christian can sometimes be a person who is against doing the Word as it relates to the Church and not realizing they are offending God by doing so. Many people do not realize that rebelling against leadership is an offense to

God, and others do not realize they are rebelling, feeling like they just have a "difference in opinion". It is one thing to disagree with the leadership; it is another thing to *always* be in disagreement. Romans 16:17 lets us know that we each have a responsibility to divisive persons. Every believer should mark the divisive person and pastors should reiterate this Word to the congregation so that even new converts will know how to do so. Pastors should confront the divisive person one to two times (Titus 3:10), and then reject them if they do not want to repent of these evil deeds. At that point, the pastor can eventually let the congregation know to avoid them (Matt.18:16-17). Many Christians may think this is a little harsh. While this may seem harsh, we have to be obedient to the word of God. It is a far better idea than anything we can conjure up! Our own opinions will never work over the Word of God, so we are better off using the principles that He lays out in His Word instead of trying to figure it out for ourselves. This is how every believer can help other Christians.

Solid Young People Make Good Leaders

Churches today are full of young people being reared in the faith. Pouring into youngsters at a young age prepares them to be excellent leaders when they begin blossoming. An angry little seven year old can become an asset to other young people up the road if a person takes time to see to the needs of the child. It can sometimes be easier to get a child to open up for emotional healing, rather than wait until they have strayed or perpetuated that same anger on others in the Church. If a young person is genuinely nurtured, he or she would be more likely to stay planted and not go off into other endeavors. They will also bring their friends, because whenever a young person knows they are being nurtured, others want "in" on the supply. Unfortunately, many youngsters come from dysfunctional homes that create a great need for mentors and those who do not mind caring for a young person. If you have young people in your church, nurture them. Sufficiently nurtured young people make excellent leaders.

This is the reason why athletic coaches are so successful. Eventually, those that were sufficiently coached and mentored become coaches and mentors themselves! A good leader will not only lead but instruct, train and encourage. This is necessary when looking over the congregation to scout out potential leaders. Be careful not to pick a young person too early; use your spiritual discernment to know when these potential leaders are ready for deliberate and intentional grooming.

The Conclusion of the Matter.

In short, choose wisely from those among you. You do not have to go outside of your assembly to choose a great leader. Sometimes the best ones are "home grown," because you know what you are getting and will have no surprises. This will also allow you to groom, counsel and nurture potential leaders at your own pace. These are the ones that are also not likely to pick up and leave if they get "better" offers when someone notices their leadership capabilities.

But the LORD said unto Samuel, Look not on his countenance, or on the height of his stature; because I have refused him: for the LORD seeth not as man seeth; for man looketh on the outward appearance, but the LORD looketh on the heart.. 1 Samuel 16:7b

Chapter Reflections

To Potential Leaders:

1. Do you find yourself keeping track of the time you are giving to the ministry?
2. Do you find yourself incessantly fighting to carve out your own time? When you receive the time you have fought for, do things work out or do they seem to go awry?
3. Do you find that you are angry or disappointed when you are not compensated or rewarded in the manner you expect?
4. Who do you talk to when you are disgruntled? Is there someone that you vent to?

Plan of Action:

You could be trying to save your life and find that you are actually losing it. Make this a matter of urgent prayer. Trust The Lord, give of yourself freely, and watch how much of your life you actually gain.

To Pastors:

1. Do you have a faithful person in place to assist you in/ with the work of the ministry?
2. In your observation, do they seem to be angry, resentful or unhappy? Consider what can be done for each of them. Do they need your counsel or Biblical Counseling?
3. As a leader, how connected are you to those around you?
4. Are people challenged and able to grow from the information that you preach or teach?

Plan of Action:

Prayerfully consider creating fellowship opportunities for those that work in the ministry with you. Create open lines of communication and room for dialogue that provokes them to be honest and transparent. Also, seek out and identify those that appear to be the stable Christians in the midst (Please note that these are only initial steps and there are other recommendations in the book that will allow you to go deeper).

But the LORD said unto Samuel, Look not on his countenance, or on the height of his stature; because I have refused him: for the LORD seeth not as man seeth; for man looketh on the outward appearance, but the LORD looketh on the heart.. 1 Samuel 16:7b

Unit II: Are They Ready For The Task?

Then he arose, and went after Elijah, and ministered unto him. 1 Kings 19:21b

-4-

Servant Leaders

Sister Alma was encouraged and very hopeful. She had begun to see so many leaders in her midst; there were leaders everywhere. She didn't feel deserted anymore, for she realized that God had been with them all along. "Why didn't my husband see this?" she mused.

There were so many from which to choose; so she began to pray again and this time she was sure to discern the right ones.

Some of these leaders were already working diligently in the midst and had hinted to helping anyway, knowing that Sister Alma needed to make decisions in this area. As she began to pray, the Lord began to speak to her spirit and impressed upon her a particular scripture. He gave her Colossians 3:22-23:

> *Servants, obey in all things your masters according to the flesh; not with eye service, as men pleasers; but in singleness of heart, fearing God: And whatsoever ye do, do it heartily, as to the Lord, and not unto men.*

"Some of these may be potential leaders," she said to herself, "but are they serving as unto the Lord or are they man pleasers?" Now she felt that she had clearer vision.

Understanding the Nature of the Man Pleaser

Ken and Jet were close friends that had worked together in ministry for approximately six years. They grew up together in a progressive Protestant church in Atlanta, Georgia. Pastor Roy was a noted speaker and one that many young men sought after for nurturing and mentoring. As Ken and Jet labored together, they soon found themselves competing with each other. They toiled arduously to please Pastor Roy, desirous of being the favored one. Neither Ken nor Jet ever had any male nurturing from their fathers, so it was important to them that they stayed in "good graces" with Pastor Roy. Things soon began to get ugly when Ken realized that Jet was getting more responsibility. Even though Ken would see Pastor Roy regularly and would often drive him to his daily appointments, Pastor Roy was soon relying on Jet to take on some of the mundane tasks and errands that he could not physically do as a result of time restraints.

These men were faithful to Pastor Roy, but not faithful to God – they were men pleasers. Their constant competition for affirmation from man ended up in disillusionment and discontent. They were continually discouraged when **they** could not measure up to their own unrealistic expectations.

Colossians 3:22 tells us that we should not serve "with eye service, as men pleasers; but in singleness of heart, fearing God".

Serving as Men Pleasers

What are the motives behind our service to others? Why do we do the things we do? Why do we choose the career paths that we have chosen? These and many other questions plague us after we find ourselves in such discouraging situations.

There is much interesting and enlightening information in a book called "High Maintenance Relationships" by Les Parrott, III, Ph.D. Men pleasers are known in his book as "chameleons." While he deals with many high maintenance relationships that we may encounter from day to day, he states this particular personality is the most deceptive in that they appear to be low maintenance at first. They do not argue and have a tendency to go with the flow. They are easy to get along with but, he says, underneath their agreeable exterior is a complex web of distorted perception and unquenchable and unappeasable longings.[xiv]

Then there are those who go to the other extreme to prove that they are not trying to please you. They work tirelessly to prove the opposite; if you want one thing, they will automatically want another. They talk to others about how much they are not people pleasers and they are very defensive; often walking around with a chip on their shoulder. They are overly deceptive because they do not want you to know that they are "needy" and will maintain their need undercover. They are desirous of being healed, but are too embarrassed and prideful to be open and honest about it.

Come Out of Hiding

Since the chameleon is a very deceptive person, they have to come out of hiding on their own. However, this does not mean that you shouldn't continue to expose it in some way or another. When seeking out a potential leader, ask yourself, does he or she have a desire to please people over God? I have listed some clues below that may be helpful.

- Is he or she eager to please?
- Does he or she have a hard time saying no to certain people?
- Does he or she have problems following through after they have made a commitment?
- Does he or she avoid conflicts with certain people?
- Does he or she get offended by certain persons very easily?
- Does he or she crave approval from certain people?
- Does he or she find it hard to make decisions on their own and consistently look for others to make the decisions for them?
- Does he or she feel as if they are not accepted?

If you find that the response to a majority of the above questions is in the affirmative, the individual is probably attempting in some way to please man. When a person is not giving genuine, honest and truthful service it is called false humility. It might look like humility on the surface, but will stink of pride underneath! Every nice gesture will be filled with their own agendas, self-gratification and self-medication. They have the desire to feed their needy and damaged emotions, pleasing you and not God.

The Apostle Paul exhorts in Colossians 3:22, "Servants, obey in all things your masters according to the flesh; not with **eye service**, as **men pleasers;** but in singleness of heart, fearing God". According to *Strong's Exhaustive Concordance,* the Greek term for the word "eye service" is *ophthalmodouleia* (NT:3783), which means something owed, (figuratively) a due; morally, a debt.[xv] *Vine's Expository Dictionary* defines *eye service* as "service performed only under the master's eye,[xvi] diligently performed when he is looking, but neglected in his absence" (Eph. 6:6). The man pleaser is giving what they think others want, for they want to be seen by their superiors doing a service owed. It is an overt effort to appease someone or "do them a favor." But it also means that it is done in their face, but not behind their back. This makes it so deceptive, and yes, ultimately a lie.

To please men is to actually "court" them as you would a lover. It is to pursue the person undercover and to study them[xvii] with the intent of giving them what they want only because you want their affections, applause or affirmation in return.

A good pastor friend of mine would often be called to minister away from his pulpit on some Sunday mornings, but was often leery of doing so. It wasn't because he did not have the help that he needed in other ministers. It was just that these other ministers proved to be useless whenever he was gone. They had many excuses for not being in place; some would even find out when he was going to be out and schedule other activities so that they, too, would be missing. If someone was needed to do a particular assignment, somehow it would never get done because these people were not dependable. When the person that they were trying to please was not in place, they could not function.

Serving to Fulfill a Need

Each of us has a need to be praised, affirmed, hailed, and loved. The need to feel important or even needed is a central human emotion and instinct. Yet there are so many people that serve in ministry looking to fulfill a need that these needs end up running the gamut. This puts us in the position of having to work through ulterior motives. The motive of the human heart attributes to the reasons why there are so many problems with leaders today. Jealousy and envy are outgrowths of this kind of service. Many people fight openly and subtly in an attempt to fulfill their needs; only later realizing that ultimately it is selfish pride at work.

In Colossians 3, verse 22, the Apostle Paul tells us to do our service with singleness of heart. We are to render the service we would do in the natural (daily serving not just in spiritual things; but in the natural or "carnal" things) in a spiritual way. We are to serve with integrity and honesty, without trying to meet the need to be needed, accepted or loved. This selfless service can be achieved when we render our service unto God. Doing the same service without pretense but with singleness of heart means we have one agenda and not two. It is done without trying to hide our true feelings, thoughts, or intentions; it means no double-dealing.

Colossians 3, Verse 25 says, "But he that doeth wrong shall receive for the wrong which he hath done: and there is no respect of persons". This means that men pleasing and eye service is wrong, no matter how you "slice" it. Theologian Adam Clarke notes,

> "It is possible for an unfaithful servant to wrong and defraud his master in a great variety of ways without being detected."[xviii] Pastors may not always know. But he that doeth wrong shall receive for the wrong which he has done; God sees him, and will punish him for his breach of honesty and trust. "Wasting, or not taking proper care of the goods of your master,"[xix] is wrong and I promise you, God resents it. And if a person is unfaithful in that which is little, he or she will be unfaithful in much, if he has opportunity; and God alone is the defense against an unfaithful servant. "God neither esteems nor despises any man because of his outward condition and

> circumstances; for there is no respect of persons with him. Every man is, in the eye of God, what he is in his soul: if holy, loved; if wicked, despised and rejected."[xx]

Sometimes this need for affirmation is very subtle. One very familiar way is being upset when our name is not called from the pulpit. Countless pastors have fumbled in this area, as many have left churches over serving in ministry and working on a particular church event without receiving recognition from the pulpit. The flesh gets much attached to applause, and if we do not receive our much-needed applause, we can become very angry and begin to shut down in our service. Don't get me wrong, there is nothing wrong with a little recognition; everyone should receive recognition for service of some sort from time to time. That is not the dilemma here. The problem comes into play when you need the recognition and are not able to function without it. You may say to yourself, "I don't need it." The only way to be certain is to allow someone to forget to call your name or announce your labor of love. You will do either one or two things:

- The first way is to get angry. This anger can swing two ways - passive, where you become quiet and perhaps even slow down from your work until you let the anger go, or *aggressive,* where you lash out sarcastically and say it.
- The second way is to find a way to tell it yourself in subtle boastful conversations. Sometimes we are so smooth and deceptive in this area that people won't even know that we are fulfilling a need.

Bragging and Boasting

Bragging and boasting is a form of haughtiness. Haughtiness is pride and God is not pleased with it. For years, I suffered in this area and one of the ways the Lord brought it to my attention was by allowing my name to be forgotten in all the major areas of my life - at work, school, church and in personal relationships. When it happens in every area, you know God is after something! We work so hard to get a reward in the form of applause and a pat on the back from men. We want to hear others say, "I approve of you," "I think you're good at what you do," and "I think you're wonderful." The feeling can be embarrassing when we hear how desperate we sound. But when a kind and pleasant remark from someone we have been looking to hear it from the most comes, the results can be like a drug that will keep us coming back for more; and it can be quite difficult to free ourselves from its grip.

The Scriptures say that the Pharisees were haughty people (Matt. 6:2-6) who were hypocrites with no relationship with Jesus. They aggressively did things publically to be heard and seen of men. If we find ourselves going in this direction, we should not expect our reward in heaven; for the Scriptures tell us that we already have it (Matt. 6:2, 5). Wouldn't it be a waste to get to heaven and find that we have already received our rewards in our desperate attempts here on earth? After all, did we take the assignment for what it would do to our ego? If this is the case, take the opportunity to humble yourself so that the Lord does not have to humble us.

Pleasing God Takes Relationship

"How can I change my motives?" you may say. It may seem particularly challenging, especially when you have spent so much time perfecting the areas and avenues that meet your need for affirmation. While the answer is simple, it is not something that comes naturally. I believe it can be found in Matthew 22:37-39:

> *37 Jesus said unto him, Thou shalt love the Lord thy God with all thy heart, and with all thy soul, and with all thy mind. 38 This is the first and great commandment. 39 And the second is like unto it, Thou shalt love thy neighbour as thyself.*

Jesus is giving the answer in simple form laid out in the text above. In this familiar passage, we already know that we should love the Lord our God and do it with all of our heart (nothing in comparison of him)[xxi], soul (with all his life, and ready to give up one's life)[xxii] and mind (one who applies himself only to know God, and His holy will).[xxiii] But when the second portion of that text tells us to love those around us as ourselves, we often find it difficult to do and wonder why. Perhaps it is because we are trying to love our neighbors as ourselves without first loving God with all of our heart, soul and mind.

It is not possible to do these things without first having a relationship with the Lord. When God becomes our all, everything begins to fall in place. This does not mean that we use God as if He is a genie. This means that it takes having a personal, intimate relationship with God. Many of us are prone to accomplish things without a relationship with God, so changing our mindset in this area may be difficult.

We live in a world today where a great deal of our advanced technology prevents us from having good, strong and honest relationships because it eliminates personal contact. But the Bible has not changed! Love will always be the more excellent way, and it takes personal contact to love.

Selfishness, which is a form of pride, is what makes us lousy servants. Its' fruit can be found throughout the ministry of leading people. From bragging, boasting and hypocrisy to whining, fretting and threats of taking one's life, the enemy is determined for us to serve with only ourselves and our needs in mind. The only solution to pride is humility.

Serving with Humility

> *Likewise, ye younger, submit yourselves unto the elder. Yea, all of you be subject one to another, and be clothed with humility: for God resisteth the proud, and giveth grace to the humble.* 1 Peter 5:5.

We do not wake up with humility; it has to be put on regularly, especially in the area of service. The Scripture also tells us that God resists the proud. Pride is the language of the flesh and therefore always shows up in the service of the Lord. From the Apostle Peter, we see that many of us are serving in ministry under the resistance of God, for we understand in this scripture there is a grace for serving that the proud will lack. This makes serving difficult and sometimes laborious. We want the grace that comes with humility (I Pet. 5:5-6), and yet we still want to be proud. It is so much better for us to humble ourselves and not have to be humbled by the Lord, which can be a humiliating experience.

The Conclusion of the Matter.

If you are grooming leaders that suffer in these areas, you must take advantage of the many opportunities to carefully teach and encourage the person in lessons on what humility looks like; because ultimately you will be helping them in the long run. There is no other way to become an effective leader! Mark 9:35 says, *"...If any man desires to be first, the same shall be last of all, and servant of all" (NKJV).* Don't just let them stay in their pride; help them.

Chapter Reflections

To Potential Leaders:

1. Are you a man pleaser or God pleaser?

2. Do you see your service as being unto God or man (Be honest with yourself)?

3. After careful observation and study, do you find that you are operating undercover with the intent to receive affections, applause or affirmation in return?

4. How do you serve when your pastor is not around? Are you faithful in doing so, or do you find your service to be laborious, boring or menial?

5. Have you ever gotten upset when you were not thanked for service rendered to the pastor or the church?

6. Have you ever left a ministry or a church? What was the reason?

7. Do you suffer from pride or haughtiness (Do you think highly of yourself and the service you provide to others)?

Plan of Action:

Examine your heart closely. Your actions will reveal the original intent and motive of your heart. If you find that your motivation has been geared towards gaining man's approval or affirmation, then it is time to change your motives. As the deer hotly pursuing water, your pant should be for The Lord. Go back to your first love and your desire to please Him above all (including yourself).

To Pastors:

1. Have you observed whether the potential leader is eager to please God or you? Do they possess or lack character, conviction or integrity?

2. Do they serve or perform? Are their actions motivated by their devotion to God or by the craving to be accepted and affirmed? Do they struggle with being rejected?

3. Do they have a hard time saying no? Do they have problems following through after making a commitment?

4. Are they easily offended by certain people? Do they avoid conflicts with certain people?

5. Do they find it hard to make decisions on their own? Do they consistently look for others to make the decisions for them?

6. Do they receive correction well?

Plan of Action:
Your plan of action should be to help people pleasers (Colossians 3:22); those who serve with eye service. Encourage them to serve with sincere motives focusing only on what the will of the Lord is. I Corinthians 3:13 helps us to understand that each man's work will be tried by fire; and the fire shall tell of what sort it is. Do not allow those who are serving in this way to stay in their pride. Love them enough to tell them they are in error.

-5-

The Call of God's Leaders

(Recognizing an Authentic Call)

Things were looking up for Grace Temple. Sister Alma realized that she was not alone and that God was with her. She was clear as to which part was His in all of this and which part was hers. Her actions no longer felt like a chore, but an assignment from God.

She looked carefully around the ministry looking for those who were not men pleasers. There were quite a few leaders that were serving diligently that didn't look like they were trying to be "front and center." Sister Alma became concerned. Suppose she thought they were leaders and these people didn't think they themselves were leaders? This could be a dilemma; so she went back to Pastor Stiff. "Every leader eventually has a call to service," he said proudly. "I remember my call as if it were yesterday."

> *"There's a way a person carries themselves when they say yes to God," he said. His words ministered to Alma and did something to her almost instantly. The tears began to flow down her cheeks. She wanted to run somewhere and talk to God right at that moment; she couldn't wait to get to her prayer closet. Sister Alma was dealing with her own call to service.*

Recognizing an Authentic Call

We read about the call of the prophets like Moses, Elijah, Elisha and Isaiah to name a few. While they vary in their situations and circumstances, there were some similarities. For instance, they were each incapable of performing the assignments given to them without divine assistance; it was necessary for the Lord to be "with them". Many had to forsake family, friends and certain ambitions to do what they were "born" to do. They all were busy working (in the things of God) and not sitting idly on the sidelines waiting for the Lord to call them. This tells us that when we are called we will be made humble, because in and of ourselves we cannot do the task without God's help. The task can only be birthed out of an intimate relationship with Him. Beware of people who claim they are called and they do not have a relationship with the Lord. If these same people want their lives (all that they are accustomed to) and are not willing to lose it for the Gospel's sake, they probably do not have a genuine call (Matthew 10:39, 16:25, Mark 10:29-30).

A divine call from God makes a person sure. This is necessary because there will be many times when one who is called may want to give up. In the Book of Jeremiah, Chapter 20, verses 7-8, it tells us that the prophet Jeremiah wanted to give up and never mention the Lord or speak in His name, but found that His Word burns in the heart like a fire. "It's like a fire in my bones!" (NLT) He knew that he had been called by God and that giving up was not an option.

In the beginning, there were many times that I did not want the assignment that the Lord had given me. However, I knew I was called and remembered the circumstances surrounding the call; and so like the prophet Jeremiah, there was no option of giving up. These days, when I get fed up, there is never a time when I want to "throw in the towel", because quitting is not part of the package that God designed for me. Instead, I work with my options; which include sometimes praying, fasting and possibly shifting things as the Holy Spirit leads.

While everyone is called to do one thing or another for God, there are those whom it is quite clear that God is calling now to be leaders in accomplishing His will. Many say God has called them but they are so misguided that they make a mess of things. There is evidence that helps one to know that there is a call from the Lord, and it does not have to be an eerie spiritual thing. This chapter will highlight some sobering characteristics that, in my humble opinion, are indicative of an authentic call.

Hearing from the Lord

Many people say they have heard from the Lord regarding a number of things: a new job, a car, a husband or wife, a new home or some type of relocation. There is scriptural proof that one can hear from the Lord concerning some things and even more specifically a call to ministry or a particular assignment. 1 Corinthians 12:11 says, "But one and the same Spirit works all..." (NKJV). This means, if a person has "heard from the Lord" concerning the things they believe the Lord is saying, then the leader should sense a little something in their spirit as well. He is not just going to speak to the one person but he will let you know a little something as well, even if it is just an inner witness in your spirit.

People should not just be allowed to tell the leader what the Lord is saying. They should tell their leader what they believe the Lord is saying and as pastors we need to judge the word (1 Cor. 14:29) and give counsel, for the Scripture tells us "in the multitude of counsel there is safety" (Prov. 11:14, 24:6). This can be somewhat hard to grasp when one is not a very spiritual leader; for it cannot be assumed that every leader is spiritual. That is why many feel as if they are being held back by leaders that they believe "do not hear God." While I don't really subscribe to that concept for various reasons, it does not have to be hopeless for those who are not in tune with God the way others believe they need to be.

Confirmations

Another important note is that a person should have some type of confirmation. We can go around saying the Lord spoke to us, but it may have been something we conjured up or something mystical that we experienced in our mind. The Lord wants us to know that we have heard from Him and He does not desire that the Word that we have been given from Him be discredited, but well received. He will therefore, work within the boundaries of Scripture to let you know for sure that He has spoken to you. One of those ways is through confirmations.

"How does that look?" you may ask? It was set up a long time ago in Scripture that by the mouth of two to three witnesses, a thing would be established (Gen.

41:32; Deut. 19:15). This train of thought concerning confirmation continues in the New Testament (Matt. 18:16, I Cor. 14:27, 29; II Cor. 13:1). If you study these scriptures, you will see that when the Lord speaks, He will confirm what He says using other witnesses. This will let you know that you are not crazy and can be sure that you have heard from the Divine and Powerful Deity, God. Many people leave marriages, jobs and ministry assignments because they have not truly heard from the Lord. Confirmations come to help us to know that God has spoken. Perhaps someone will come to you and say they had a dream, or another will come to you and say that the Lord spoke to them and/or gave them a vision about the very thing that the Lord has told you. It is especially powerful when the person whom God uses is not a close friend, but one who may not know you so personally. God can and will do this, and if you find yourself going in this direction, you will make fewer mistakes.

If your worst member came to you and said they believe the Lord has "called them" to do something, it is obvious that it is a little ridiculous that the Lord can "speak" to them about a call and not their nasty behavior. Help that person understand this by saying it. Don't think it in your mind and not verbalize it to this potential leader. Every one of us has some kind of flaw in our character that we should be working on. It's called the fruit of the Spirit; but these same people would rather work on gifts, and not the fruit of the Spirit. This does not mean that if you communicate your wisdom to the person that they may want to go forth anyway, but at least you did not withhold this important information from them.

There are so many people in Christendom today that have erred and strayed from God's plan and ended up regretful that their leaders did not say anything to them. It was much later on that they realized just how "off" they really were. We, as pastors, owe it to potential leaders to see the traps and deception in their paths and warn them. While they may not be too excited by your warnings, the one who is really serious about God will eventually see it and thank you later.

I once counseled a person whose pastor did not see her prophetic gifting because she was the church gossiper. This person was very insecure and wanted to be accepted by everyone around her; so when she got a word in prayer she would share it with others to boast indirectly that God spoke to her. A great deal of the time, she compromised people's personal information in doing so. Sometimes she was very much on point, but sometimes it was speculation based on what she heard from the friends that she talked to for several hours over the phone. Her name came up several times in the scandalous situations in the church. It became such an issue that her pastor had to chide her to mind her own business. So when she brought words "from the Lord" she was not credible, and when she was looking to be taken more seriously in the ministry, it did not happen. She was considered untrustworthy mainly because she worked on spiritual gifts, and not the fruit of the spirit. Jesus says in Matthew 12:33, "Either make the tree good, and his fruit good; or else make the tree corrupt, and his fruit corrupt: for the tree is known by his fruit". We have a responsibility to make ourselves into "trees of righteousness."

Clarke notes, "The works will resemble the heart: nothing good can proceed from an evil spirit; no good fruit can proceed from a corrupt heart. Before the heart of man can produce any good, it must be renewed and influenced by the Spirit of God."[xxiv]

Seeing the Call on Others

Many potential leaders are sitting in the pew waiting for us to "get a clue". However, sometimes we cannot sense the Lord prodding us because we are too busy saying that we can't visualize the person in that light. A great deal of things can begin to happen around you until you finally see that God is speaking very loudly. One that has budding possibility will wait on God to show you, which takes great humility to do, and He will; while others may begin to step out in faith hoping their leaders will believe it when they see it.

This means it is important to stay open to the Lord regarding the use of His people. Sometimes our own intimidation or mental obstacles can get in the way of hearing, sensing or even seeing what God is saying regarding the people that He has placed in our care.

If you have put people to work in the service of the Lord, it is always easier to watch for potential leaders. However there will be some that will be inactive and will eventually come to you and say that they sense a call to ministry or service of some kind. When these potential leaders come to you and say the Lord has called them, begin to put them to work right away so that you can begin watching them differently. Give them assignments to serve in the ministry so that you will have opportunity to see them in action. You will be able to see how well they work under leadership, how well they follow instructions and carry out someone else's vision before someday carrying their own, and sometimes it will allow you to see the person's call more clearly. If you see resistance in the willingness of a person to submit to your vision, more than likely things will not get much better until healing in that particular area has taken place. That same stubborn person will eventually look to leave your congregation and follow his or her own pursuits without submitting to anyone else's authority. If you show them where they are erring from the Scriptures it may be a little easier for them to handle, knowing they must live by the

Scriptures. However, if this person's heart is fixed on doing what it wants, do not look for any loyalties.

Here are some practical ways that one can assess another's call to ministry of some sort.

1. Does this person love God and seek to please God in their endeavors and pursuits or do they seek to promote their own personal gain?

As stated earlier, many people do not have the time to carry another person's vision, especially if they think they know a little about their own vision. Deception can entice a person to go on their own and it can fool even the best of us. Walking in servanthood and humility means first serving others until that time is up, and only God knows when that time is. It is then that He will promote you. 1 Peter 5:6 says, "Humble yourselves therefore under the mighty hand of God, that he may exalt you in due time"

2. Does this person's life portray just as much spiritual fruit as spiritual gifts?

Many can flourish in the gifts of the spirit; however, these same people can have problems blossoming in the fruit of the spirit, which can make for a frustrating situation. People are enthralled by gifts and assume that the fruit is in place. Many leaders today can confront people about stepping out in the gifts of the spirit, but are intimidated when it comes to encouraging people to step out in the fruit of the spirit.

3. Does this person follow leadership?

This is slightly different from carrying a person's vision. It means can they submit to the vision of the leadership of the church. Sometimes, it does not always mean the potential leader has another vision or agenda, it may simply mean that he or she has submission problems; submission to authority. Frankly speaking the question is "Are they rebellious?" Many of us do not like that word because it seems a little harsh. However, that is the subtle deception that the enemy uses so that the person would not be apt to change. Rebellious people do not have to be very blatant in their doings; not doing what you ask is a form of rebellion. The deceptive ones have "good" excuses, or should I say reasons, for doing their own thing. Take Saul, for example, who did not do exactly what he was told to do in I Samuel 15:24. The reasoning he gave for his doings was that he feared the people. He chose the people over God! Therefore, he could not be trusted to carry out God's plan.

4. Is this person respected in the church, (especially among their peers)? If not why not?

A person's track record and how they are viewed in the eyes of the other parishioners is a very important sign of whether or not a person has been called. How well do they work with others? Are they destructive in their relationships? If so, things will not get better because a person is "called". This type of behavior pattern should be brought to the attention of the potential leader so that they will know what the weak areas are that need work. Promoting task oriented people without assisting them in this area would only set a person up for great failure. We as pastors and leaders owe it to a person who may be ailing to groom them in God's way of working with people (whether these people are potential souls or saints). The potential soul is most important to God and He is equally concerned about the treatment of the saints. This doesn't mean that a person who does not get along with others is not generally called; it just means that putting them in position can do more harm than good. Sometimes some biblical counseling is necessary.

5. Does this person's family agree that there is a sign of a calling? Can family members attest to the godly character that is displayed in public?

A person's immediate family (spouse and children) can usually tell you whether they are in agreement with a call from the Lord. Many have been "called" to minister in God's house and the home situations were not very impressive. It is important to ask yourself, what is this person doing as a result of the difficulties in the home situation? If they are ignoring the situations, avoiding them or justifying them, it is safe to assume that they will tackle the ministry's problems the same way. As noted previously, God still calls those that are less than perfect, but we are still admonished to "lay aside the weights and sins that so easily beset us" (Heb. 12:1). This means we need to encourage those potential candidates that cannot seem to wait for God to change people or even situations. If they are not able to see or recognize problems or disasters in their own homes, ask their children or their spouses about their family life. If those family members are honest, each will appreciate the concern and give you the answers that you are seeking. They may be a little twisted and perhaps even blown out of proportion in some areas, but nevertheless these situations should not be ignored. Home situations need to be resolved or be in the process of being resolved for a person striving to do well in ministry.

6. Does this person successfully hold a fulltime job?

Work ethics play a great part in leadership ability; if they will submit themselves to an earthly system, then your potential leader has the ability to submit to God's system. A person's character is displayed in how they give a day's work to the boss. If the person has a different job every few weeks, or if they do not find themselves working on a regular basis (depending on the reasons why) determines whether or not this same person will be consistent in ministry. If ethics and responsibility is unable to motivate them to go to a secular job on a regular basis to earn a weekly salary, pushing past their flesh to submit to the service of ministry will not prove profitable either. Sure it may look hopeful, but eventually the same things that make them inconsistent will make them inconsistent again. It is necessary to find out why this potential leader struggles in this area. Once you have helped him to find out, you may have done more for them than you will ever know.

If you cannot answer any of the questions listed above favorably, it is safe to assume that you will have problems with your potential candidate. Keep in mind that God is not calling perfect people! He is calling for those who are looking to be complete in Him.

A Genuine call

Many times we feel that we have been called, but that call may not necessarily be a call to leadership or ministry. It may just be a call to get closer to God! We must not mistake a wooing of the Holy Spirit to get more intimate with God for a call to ministry. If we step out under this impression, the results can be devastating.

Dr. Nathan, a pastor friend of mine, had a young man in his church that was popular with the young people. This young man would enthrall the hearts of many as he spoke about the things God was doing in his life and how he was called to ministry. However this young man was rebellious and would not do the things that were required by the church because he had an inner vow that nobody would tell him what to do. Therefore, he did not follow rules. Dr. Nathan did not wish to make a mess of things and ordained him thinking to himself that it would possibly ground the young man and perhaps form a relationship between the two of them. Instead this young minister started his own work within the church and eventually started a church of his own in a building not far from the church.

He took several young persons from the church with him and began leading them away from God into a life of compromise until he suffered an asthma attack and died suddenly in his home during the wee hours of the morning several weeks later. What a break for Dr. Nathan when many of his young people came flooding back into the congregation after having left for a few short weeks.

This is not to say that you should ignore those who believe they are called when they have character flaws, but it does say more grooming, mentoring and healing should take place before you put someone in a position of power as they can lead the sheep astray even without leaving the actual building!

The Conclusion of the Matter

Take the time to get to know your people so that when the Lord speaks you can be in tune with what He is actually saying. This way when your potential leader comes to you and tells you what they believe the Lord is saying you can be available to assist them in their process (and not support them in their mess) to be all that God has called them to be.

Chapter Reflections

To Potential Leaders:

1. Do you honestly feel inadequate for the task at hand or could this be a "false humility"?

2. Have you heard the Lord call you to a particular ministry in the church? How has He confirmed the call?

3. Have you ever been wrong (regarding hearing from The Lord) concerning a major situation in your life? If so, what did you do afterwards and how has that affected you today?

4. Is your call to your local body or anywhere you want to go?

5. Does your leader see your call as well?

Plan of Action:

Here's what you do… Go to your leader and share what you believe you have heard. Include scripture verses and confirmations from others (credible) as well (if any).

To Pastors:

1. Have you seen or bore witness to a call in a potential leader?

2. Have you spoken to this person (even if they are the worst member)?

3. Is their call to the church or their own ministry?

4. Are they able to follow you and carry your vision or are they only interested in pursuing their vision?

5. Do you witness in them the Fruit of the spirit (This is a big part of a call)?

6. Do they follow leadership? Are they disciplined or rebellious? Do they have other agendas?

7. What is their track record? What positive and/or negative things are they known for?

8. What does their family say about them? Is biblical counseling necessary for this person in order to meet the standard?

Plan of Action:

Make a list of potential leaders. How possible is it that the Lord has called these individuals? How good or bad is the character of the called persons? What is your plan to assist them in coming out of an ungodly character? Commit to the time necessary on your part to bring them up to par and allow God to do His part. Do not put them in place until you are sure that they are ready to start moving in God's direction. Stay prayerful and do not move too prematurely.

-6-
No Novices

Among the many people that Sister Alma considered, Justice Turner or "Turner" as he was known was high on her list of candidates. But Turner did not seem to be as settled as he should be. While he was faithful, his desire to settle into the ministry work on another level would compete with his family's ambitions for him; and he wanted to please his family equally as much as he wanted to work for the ministry. He was young and not familiar with commitment on the level that Sister Alma was interested in; so she wondered if her choice to put Turner in place would backfire. "Perhaps I could get him licensed as a minister and put him in place administratively in the church office," she thought to herself. Maybe the thought of getting ordained would lure him into making a strong commitment on this end and surely the thought of being ordained would surpass Turner's feelings of pleasing his family.

This is a true saying, If a man desire the office of a bishop, he desireth a good work... 6 Not a novice, lest being lifted up with pride he fall into the condemnation of the devil.

1 Tim 3:1, 6

The Selection Process – No Novices!

1Timothy 3 instructs us that we can find leaders and still find ourselves compromising in our selection of them so it is necessary for us to have a check list. One such list is given to us in this chapter. Verse six in this chapter says, if a person desires the office of an overseer it is important that the person not be a novice. When seeking out potential leaders, this scripture can be very helpful. I know that you may have understood a novice to mean a beginner or even a new convert and you may want to bypass this particular chapter, but I encourage you to read further because I have come to understand in my short time of leadership and working with leaders that the word novice is not fully researched so that we may know its full meaning. When choosing leaders we must be careful to have full knowledge of what a novice looks like so that we do not run into problems up the road.

What is a Novice?

The word novice in the Greek is the word "neophutos" as in "neophyte". When we think of the word neophyte we think of a newly converted person, one who is new to a particular belief system, almost as a heathen or a step above a nonbeliever. In the early church it was one who was newly baptized. [xxv] In subsequent years, the Church felt it wise to put converts under a course of instruction before admitting them to baptism and the full privileges of Christian brotherhood, and this term was sometimes applied to them as well.

Historical Novices

The interesting thing about this is that the term novice was originally the label given to persons of either sex who were living in a monastery, in a state of probation, prior to becoming professed members of a monastic order. The persons who apply to enter this particular state, "on being admitted by the superior of the monastery, promise obedience to him during the time of their stay," and these people were bound to conform to the discipline of the house. They would make no permanent vows, and had the option of leaving should they find that the monastic life did not suit them.[xxvi]

This period of the novitiate would not be less than one year and those who entered had to be past the age of puberty. The married persons could not be admitted unless they both had consented; so that the spouses could not be a hindrance to the demands made by the monastery. The person was not allowed to be encumbered with a great deal of debts and could not be those whose assistance was necessary for the support of his or her parents. Widowers and widows could be admitted as long as their labor was not required for the support of their children. After the completion of the year of probation, the novice, "if he (or she) persists in his vocation, and his conduct and capacity had proven satisfactory", would be admitted into the order by taking the "solemn vows", which were binding for life. Some monasteries even cautioned against admitting novices without a full examination of their disposition, morals, and mental and bodily qualifications.[xxvii]

Such is the case with those called to discipleship in Christ. We are instructed in Luke 14:28 to count the cost. This does not mean that we are to wait a year to see if we want to go God's way, but we are to enter into the life of discipleship knowing what to expect. Luke 9:59 and Matthew 8:21 speaks of one who wanted to follow Jesus but asked if he could wait until his father passed on before taking on such a task. To many, this could have seemed to be a most reasonable and noble request since respect for parents, living or dead, is one of the first duties of religion. But Jesus saw that in his circumstances, perhaps if he were permitted to go, he possibly would get distracted and not return. So He commanded him to execute the more important duty, that of attending to the salvation of souls, even at the risk of the very apparent neglect of another duty. Could this example further explain to us that the first duty of man is the saving of souls, and everything else should be made subordinate to that?[xxviii]

Beware of Novices

A struggling pastor searched his congregation for a minister to take over his prayer ministry at the church. He had been watching a particular young lady named Berta who had been with the ministry several years and was hoping he could get her to take on this endeavor. She wasn't one who really stood out in the crowd as being very spiritual or anything of the sort, but she was always in the Church, so he felt that was a start. She had also been raised in the Church. But upon examining her more closely, he discovered she was comfortable with being 'in' the Church but not necessarily comfortable with living biblically. She was not really interested in what the word said about the life of a Christian and her poor life choices and constant move from one job to another made that fact very evident.

This same pastor decided to go with Brother Jesse who was more of an older, quiet and gentle sort of person. He was not as outgoing as Berta and he wasn't in Church as often as she was, but he did seem a great deal more responsible. Without hesitation he made the decision to place Jesse over the ministry of prayer in the church. A few short months later he realized the prayer ministry had not been flourishing at all. He called Bro. Jesse in to talk about how things could get better; Bro. Jesse quickly nodded in agreement to the changes and went on his way. The following week he found that Jesse was missing from the Sunday morning service. This was not odd since in the past he was not as regular as other members. But he became concerned when three weeks passed and he still had not heard from or seen him. He sought out those who knew him thinking that maybe he was sick or ailing in some way; only to find out that Bro. Jesse had decided to take his membership elsewhere; stating "this is what the Lord told him to do".

After trying incessantly to meet with Bro. Jesse in person, he finally had the opportunity to speak with him over the phone. Bro. Jesse did not see anything wrong with how he handled his decision to move his membership and was not open to the counsel from the leader. He was only interested in attending a church with a "larger music ministry".
Many pastors are not initially privy to the reasons why people make the decisions to leave a ministry or any other fickle decisions that they make. Just as the monasteries of old knew what things could "trip a person up", we as pastors also understand the distractions of those who have not counted the cost of discipleship (Luke 14:28).

In summary, what I have learned in my experiences and noting the restrictions of the ancient views of novices, I have come to a definition of my own regarding novices. If you adhere to my counsel in this area, you probably will not have as many problems in the area of putting leaders in place. I have listed it below.

Hearers Only

First and foremost a person who is not well versed in the Scriptures will not be able to fully live by the Scriptures. Ask yourself, do they place themselves in positions at the church where they can receive the sincere milk of the word so that they can grow in the Scriptures (I Pet. 2:2)? A person who hungers and thirst after righteousness are the ones that will be filled (Matt. 5:6) and if this person is showing signs of a love for the Word of God they are on their way to spiritual growth in the Lord. Please understand that a person can be in the Church for years and not have a love for the Word of God. It is not until you see this beginning to take shape that you can trust that these persons have plans to become a doer of the word (Jam. 1:23). If the person is open to learning the Scriptures, that you may note the individual's transformation, I still caution you to be sure that you are diligent in your press to teach them the Scriptures as you begin. A desire to learn the word does not always constitute definite results.

Constantly Moving

Another way to find out whether or not you have a novice is to check to see if this person has stayed on a job for more than one year without moving around. This could be a sign of discontentment and possibly even poor character. If a person is discontented, they will always find reasons as to why they cannot stay in their present position. If they do not stay in positions on the job, the likelihood is that they will not sustain a position in the church either. Are they trying in some way to fulfill a need of some sort? And when doing so, they will find themselves constantly searching for something else to fill the need after the initial excitement wears off. I myself never stayed on certain secular jobs very long but my track record in the house of the Lord was very different. I was fashioned for ministry and it was quite evident since I was blossoming there. This can differ if the person is more interested in working in ministry over the secular community, but this character flaw can be a deadly one so be careful.

Some who have not yet made the decision to abandon their dreams to follow after what God has planned for them will either try to incorporate their dream in your endeavor or will leave when they believe they see an opportunity that embraces their dreams. When it comes to our own passions and desires, many who are spiritually immature may find themselves leaving the ministry to run after these passions and desires at the most inopportune time.

Unstable Married persons

Beware of married persons, who make decisions without their spouse's consent as this could be signs of an ailing marriage. I can assure you it won't take long before that same person will either change their minds because of the same spouse; or find that they had the wrong motive for serving in the ministry and adjust it at the time when it is least expected. An ailing marriage can also be signs of a person or persons who are struggling in the area of being a doer of the Word (Jam. 1:3-25). If they struggle with being a doer of the word in their home, that is something that needs to be conquered before thrusting them into ministry and looking for them to tackle difficult situations. Marriage is good training ground for ministry and spiritual growth.

Financial Responsibilities

One who is the sole person financially responsible for the support of children must be careful not to consistently drop the disciplines of the ministry to fulfill the demands of that responsibility. To ask someone to choose between the demands of ministry and the responsibility of acquiring additional jobs, or extra hours, to secure the bread that feeds their children would not be fair. This can also be said for those who are in extreme debt.

The Selfish Mindset

Just as babies do not consider others when they want their needs met, novices can't always see the bigger picture until it is right up on them. Many times they make their decisions out of selfish desires. Sometimes these desires are masked and we do not see the puffing up of the flesh because the reasons for the flakiness can be so subtle. Jesus said in Luke 9:62, "No man, having put his hand to the plough, and looking back, is fit for the kingdom of God".

Such persons are also known as fickle persons; which means "deceitful". They are deceivers that are associated with hostility and anger. It is marked by lack of steadfastness, constancy, or stability: given to erratic changeableness. Examples of such would be one who is characterized by instability, especially with regard to affections or attachments; or one who "chases" someone they so want badly but dislikes the person once they like you back; and finally, one who experiments with or messes around with people.[xxix] Sometimes a person may have a genuine call but their behavior shows signs of instability and fickleness.

Pastor Paul, a successful pastor of a very prosperous ministry, was looking for a youth pastor to lend leadership to their growing and thriving youth ministry. Well spoken and accomplished, Derk was a sure fit; he certainly had the credentials and a definite "call on his life". You can imagine their dismay when not long after taking the position Derk was constantly pursuing the young women in the ministry and changing his mind every few months.

Our same scripture in I Tim. 3 tells us that a novice will be lifted up with pride, and the result will be the falling into the condemnation of the devil.

The International Standard Bible Encyclopedia puts it this way, a novice runs the very serious risk of being wise in his own eyes and of despising those who are still on the level from which, by his conversion, he has been lifted. This person is sure to become puffed up with his high and fleshly ideas of his own importance. A novice may not yet have discovered their limitations, and does not fully comprehend his true position in the "Christian community." For these and other reasons, he is liable to instability, other weaknesses and sins connected with it. All of his pride is a "sure indication of a coming fall". A novice, therefore, would surely bring disgrace upon the position of leadership.[xxx]

The Conclusion of the Matter: Count The Cost!

So what does this mean? Does it mean that these people cannot serve as leaders? God forbid. Many of us as pastors have put novices in place and did not think that we would suffer. We put them in positions we thought they could handle and sometimes things eventually worked itself out; but not usually without some sort of humiliation, even in its slightest form. I believe it just means that there should be a resolve in the heart of both the pastor and the potential leader regarding these things. Luke 14:28 says, "For which of you, intending to build a tower, sitteth not down first, and counteth the cost, whether he have sufficient to finish it?" It does not say that you should not build, but you should consider what you have to give up in order that you may complete the building. A spiritually mature person will have a resolve and would not compromise either situation in order to get the tasks done. If you see a candidate for leadership that looks promising, do the check and see if you find that they are lacking in the areas mentioned.

If you believe, and are sure that the Lord is prompting you to choose a novice, do not get angry when the pitfalls come into play for the Lord may be using it to grow you up! Work at bringing that person to their full potential. The results can be rewarding.

Then he arose, and went after Elijah, and ministered unto him. 1 Kings 19:21b

Chapter Reflections

To Potential Leaders:

1. Do you believe that you are being "passed over" in the areas of leadership selection because you are not adequate in the areas of experience or age?

2. What are some of the mistakes you have made in the ministry (this includes personal mistakes) that may be disqualifying you for certain areas of ministry in the church.

3. Are there any areas cited in this chapter that you may need to become stronger in so that you can be ready to take on the demands of ministry?

Plan of Action:

Set up an appointment with your pastor and tell him you would like to assist in the work of the ministry in any area that he or she sees fit. Let him know the areas that you see as weak in your life and ask him for any other weak spots he may have noticed. Together, work on a plan to "mature" in that area and stay accountable to your pastor until those areas become solid.

To Pastors:

1. Has any of the information in this chapter caused you to note any potential novices?

2. What is your plan (as much as depends on you) to bring those persons to reach their potential?

3. Do you have a track record of picking novices?

Plan of Action:

If you are struggling with a large amount of novices perhaps you can institute a spiritual growth program in your church and make it mandatory for those leaders (or potential leaders) to attend; so they can get started identifying their flaws and working towards growth. If it is just a few persons perhaps recommending some biblical counseling for a season to work through "stuck" places may be helpful.

Then he arose, and went after Elijah, and ministered unto him. 1 Kings 19:21b

-7-

Team Players

("Can't We All Just Get Along?")

Sharla and Thomas were at it again and as always, Pastor Tray was mediating yet another incident between them in an effort to get them to work out their differences. Sharla was married for 10 years to Rev. Nance and Thomas was newly married for two years to Renee Leake. They worked together in the media ministry for three years and it just seemed that things never got better between them.

Thomas spearheaded the actual production of the merchandise while Sharla was responsible in overseeing the volunteers. "He never communicates!" Sharla shouted emotionally, always letting her emotions rule the situation. "I feel like, I feel like!" she explained over and over again. This was the phrase with which she began every grievance that came from her lips".

"Can't We All Just Get Along?"

Thomas was an avoider who would shut down and not deal with the conflicts that came about. His reasoning was that Sharla and some of the other women on the team were "so controlling and so emotional". Although Sharla and Thomas appeared to be faithful to their marriages and their positions at the church, the incidents would occur again and again but it just seemed that they were never able to resolve conflicts without a great deal of mediation. If Pastor Tray didn't intervene, things would never get resolved.

This situation may sound familiar to you; many pastors find themselves unnecessarily mediating the same problems over and over. Just like with some marriages, it may seem as if things will never change. I always say, "You have to know what you're working with" and see it ahead of time. Sharla came to the ministry broken and dysfunctional having been verbally and physically abused by her father; and Thomas was the victim of a very controlling mother. They were always feeling like victims when conflicts came about. These issues were not worked through and as a result, conflicts—and there were many—would always end in Sharla wanting to quit and Thomas walking away stating "he doesn't have to deal with this".

Pastor Tray was disgusted that he had to deal with the same issues over and over; "When was it going to change?" he thought. If he knew this was going to take place every week he would never had made them leaders in the media ministry. They were easily offended and always whining like victims, but they were good at what they did in the ministry.

This is a common problem in the church; skills and gifts are in abundance, but good character and emotional healing is scarce. Pastors do not deal with it too much anymore, but it doesn't stop them from having to deal with the consequences of that scarcity. Working with people that are struggling in their emotions is like dealing with children. Unless you help them to heal and grow both spiritually and emotionally, you will always have to combat the same issues over and over again.

There were similar problems in the Corinthian church. First Corinthians is divided into Paul's discussions of the various problems that existed in the Corinthian church. The entire book, beginning in verse 10 of chapter 1, deals with the problems in the assembly. It gives a contrast between the foolishness of men (which they think is wisdom), and the wisdom of God (which they think is foolishness). In other words, it contrasts human wisdom with divine wisdom. We all have our own philosophy of how things should be done. Many of these philosophies are belief systems that we have learned through the years in order to cope with our circumstances. These viewpoints and values are the ways in which we handle conflicts and govern our decision making. They exalt itself against the knowledge of God in our lives (2 Cor. 10:5).

As a result, the church became split into little groups, each holding various philosophical viewpoints. This is because even though they became Christians, they still held on to their particular philosophy. Instead of handling situations according to our own philosophy, we should handle our problems biblically – how God wants us to handle things. These are the things that pastors should promote but we as pastors are not always comfortable confronting people. Among many reasons, popularity and fear of being called controlling (the deceptive phrase used by many) has paralyzed countless pastors today. It is a trick of the enemy to get us to abandon our responsibility of shepherding God's flock and as a result the Christians of today are running amuck. We have rendered the intervention of leadership immobile because we do not want anyone to challenge us.

First Corinthians, chapter two and verses 12-16 in the New Living translation paraphrases it so eloquently when it says, "God has actually given us his Spirit (not the world's spirit)"...Paul says, "When we tell you this, we do not use words of human wisdom. We speak words given to us by the Spirit, using the Spirit's words to explain spiritual truths. But people who are not Christians cannot understand these truths from

God's Spirit. It all sounds foolish to them because only those who have the Spirit can understand what the Spirit means". Others cannot understand this and how could they? They do not have the mind of Christ.

Why Can't We Just Get Along?

These wrangling(s) are considered the works of the flesh, which are: hatred, variance, emulations, wrath, **strife,** seditions, **envyings**" (Gal 5:20-21). They had demonstrated these things in their divisions; and Paul therefore addressed them according to their character knowing that their danger lay in this direction.

In chapter three of Galatians, we understand that the reason why they found themselves quarreling with each other is because they were carnal; equivalent to those who do not know the Lord. Paul adds that these people are not even able to handle the Word of God (which in this case is Godly counsel) because they are just like babes. The difference is that they were babes who could not even hold solid milk in their spiritual systems. The Scripture says, *"ye were not able to bear it, neither yet now are ye able."* Have you ever experienced a baby who could not digest milk? The mothers have to constantly switch the formulas so that the babies can eventually get the nourishment that they need. Carnal people are not really interested in receiving scripture but rather are interested in getting their worldly philosophies and opinions across. They are committed to these opinions and will wrestle with you to hold onto them. As a pastor, it can be very taxing to deal with such persons, but we must be committed to the Word of God and to getting the Word into them.

It is normal to see a baby drinking milk from a bottle, but it is abnormal to see a full grown person drinking from a bottle. This is also called dysfunctionalism. We should never settle for carnality in the church and Pastors should never allow people to do so.

Handling Carnal Christians

But what did Paul do? Did He ignore the carnal people in the church? Did he allow them to divide up into splinter groups within the church because he did not feel comfortable confronting them? The answer is in our scripture listed below:

> *1 Cor 3:1-2 And I, brethren, could not speak unto you as unto spiritual, but as unto carnal, even as unto babes in Christ. I have fed you with milk, and not with meat: for hitherto ye were not able to bear it, neither yet now are ye able.*

Paul is admonishing us firstly not to treat them as if they are spiritual for it will only frustrate you. Lower your expectations because they are unrealistic. *Hebrews 5:11-14 says, "While we may have many things to say, they are hard to be uttered, because you are dull of hearing. These people ought to be teachers but need to be taught again the basics. And as a result of the constant need for milk and not strong meat they are unskilled in the word of righteousness" (ESV).* If you begin to speak to them as if they are spiritually mature, your words would sound like foolishness to these people, ultimately frustrating yourself in the process.

Scripture says to treat them as new converts who are new to the things of God. We should remember that even though they may not want the milk, we must be consistent and pray that they will eventually take it and crave for spiritual milk more and more! We should pray that they begin to cry "out for the nourishment as a baby cries for milk" (I Peter 2:2 NLT).

The Conclusion of the Matter

In short, Pastors must beware! We have a tendency to ordain and/or empower carnal people for ministry and wonder why they give us such a hard time. Do not expect a carnal person to be spiritually mature. Be realistic about what to expect from them and be ready at all times to consistently intervene in their setbacks with the sincere milk of the word, and not strong meat, so that they do not choke.

Chapter Reflections

To Potential Leaders:

1. Do you find yourself consistently grumbling to others (or perhaps just to leadership) about different ones in the ministry with which you seemingly cannot get along?

2. Are you in agreement with someone who consistently grumbles in this area?

3. What are some of the areas where you find problems consistently showing up?

Plan of Action:

Romans 12:18 says, "As much as lieth in you live peaceably with all men". Develop a plan to work peaceably with those that you seem to have regular conflicts with. Consult with a seasoned mentor or leader to confirm that the conflicts have occurred more than one or two times, since we are not always honest with ourselves. Do not consider leaving or giving up in that area of ministry. This should not be one of your options. If you are still struggling with solutions talk to your leadership about some counsel in this area.

To Pastors:

1. Do you or others constantly have to intervene in on conflicts between the same people most of the time? Is it a reoccurring problem with one person in particular?

2. Have you confronted these individuals? What was the outcome?

3. Is Biblical counseling necessary?

Plan of Action:

Do not avoid striving with others in the area of conflicts; many have not learned the art of conflict resolution. Scripture however, contains specific instructions regarding this matter. Point them to the scriptures. Some may not be open to the way of scripture but it is important that you be insistent. The end result will be a "weeding out" of those that do not desire God's way and those who do.

Then he arose, and went after Elijah, and ministered unto him. 1 Kings 19:21b

-8-

Nurturing Leaders

A few months before Pastor Seymour died; a discouraged and disgruntled Jocinda Mills came to see me. Over the past few years, she was excited about the fact that she felt the Lord calling her to ministry. She spoke to her pastor, the late Pastor Seymour before he passed away, and he agreed. He promised to support her in this area, but he never seemed to have the time.

He was so busy doing his ministry that he didn't have time to help her and other budding ministers in Grace Temple church. She felt so inadequate and ill prepared; she sobbed hopelessly in my office talking about the countless times that she expected to receive information from him and she was left with broken promises and unfulfilled expectations.

Failure to Nurture

Pastor Nicholas Tane, a well known speaker and noted author, was the pastor of a progressive church. People would come from miles to hear his dynamic speaking, and countless others purchased his books. He became an overnight success and those who flocked to his church did so in hopes that they would be connected to him in some way. They also desired that he would duplicate himself through them. The place was crawling with young budding men and women hoping to be a part of the dynasty. They soon found out that what they desired was not going to happen. Pastor Nick (as he was affectionately called) never made time to groom anyone and if anyone came to him for some kind of nurturing or mentoring, he made promises that were almost always broken. The people started thinking that he was mean and unfair. Many began to dislike him and eventually left the church bewildered and disillusioned. In this area, the church became a "revolving door".

Pastor Nick had people that could organize and put conferences together so that he could teach and others who could do great in praise and worship. He even had a powerful team of people that could sell the tapes and assist him in writing the books. His team was tremendous! They were sharp, quick and hopeful for some type of mentoring or grooming. But it never came. His congregation suffered also because Pastor Nick never really connected with his people. The church was large and needed leadership but he simply refused to groom someone to assist him in this area. While a few members eventually left, others stayed to continue receiving the wonderful words of encouragement in his dynamic sermons. This is a common scenario in many churches today.

Pastor Seymour and Pastor Nick are like so many pastors we know. Underneath their powerful and successful ministry, we find a very insecure, self-centered and selfish person. They may have felt very insecure about their ministries. They also did not know how to pour into (groom) anyone because possibly no one ever poured into them. Sometimes these leaders do not wish to share the attention and applause that they receive from the people with anyone else. They crave the applause and the accolades as if it were a drug! Everything in the ministry revolved around the desire to grow the audience with their wonderful words of encouragement in their sermons.

God's Grooming

I am sure that the preceding story sounds familiar to you and I must tell you that God never calls anyone without giving them some kind of preparation. The path that He has chosen for you will include, in some way, what is needed to train you for the assignment for which He has called you to. This is called Divine assistance. We understand David had this assistance in First Samuel 17:34-37. While caring for his father's sheep he was being prepared for the assignment to take down Goliath. Before the giant Philistine, he wrestled with a lion and a bear. He knew the Lord delivered him from the paws of the lion and the bear and as a result he trusted that God would do the same with the giant Philistine. God's grooming will always let us know that He is with us. If your pastor never lifts a finger to groom you, God is already grooming you in ways that are innumerable.

God knew the direction Moses had to take so he preserved him in the house of Pharaoh and eventually gave him a burden for the Egyptians with a fierce call to stand up to Pharaoh and lead the children of Israel out of bondage. He did not get any classes or special grooming for that! It could be that he was being groomed when he became Pharaoh's daughter's son though. He was possibly being nurtured in the way of leadership when she reared him, but Moses did the God-given job without training courses.

Elisha was trained by serving Elijah. While there were schools for the prophets; Elisha's double portion was coming from watching and serving Elijah very closely. Sometimes our training will come from serving the very one that will not train us. Elijah's mantle was not really His to give up for it is God who determines who gets what (I Kings 19:16). Even if you have a pastor that refuses to groom you, God is the one who is in charge. We must never fall back on thinking that our fate or future is in the hands of anyone or anything else but God. But I will add leaders do not become good leaders without help. God does his part, we as pastors and potential leaders should do our part.

So far I have been addressing those that would develop God's leaders, but let me talk for a minute to those who desire to be nurtured and developed. This may also include those pastors who never felt they, themselves, were nurtured.

God calls and equips us. He takes us through tribulation that works patience and trials that make us strong (Rom. 5:3, Jas 1:3, 1 Pet. 4:12), selecting specifically those things needed for our journey. Since the godly must suffer persecution (2 Tim. 3:12), He carefully chooses the suffering necessary for our well being; Christians do not lack in the area of suffering! He then places you in the churches and the ministries where He wants you to serve and we as pastors should take it from there. He never leaves you or forsakes you. He is always there to guide you, comfort you and give you insight through His Holy Spirit, but He will never do your job for you. Do not sit and wait for Him to do something that you, yourself should be doing. God will not cross boundaries. Don't get me wrong, you cannot ordain yourself. But God who sees and knows everything will see to it that you get ordained at the appropriate time.

Grooming and Nurturing

A good number of pastors today have problems nurturing leaders because many times they themselves have not been successfully nurtured. While it does take patience to nurture, it also takes time to nurture. This is a selfless act that can be profitable to any ministry if a pastor puts in the time. Though many leaders are not opposed to nurturing, they are not always committed to it. Nurturing takes work that does not always look profitable. Sometimes things look a little hopeless but eventually you will see the budding of a plant sprouting up in your potential leader. It can be hard sometimes to recognize when we are being nurtured. And maybe we have even been nurtured and we don't realize it because we do not know what nurturing looks like.

According to the Merriam Webster dictionary, "to nurture" is to supply with nourishment, to educate, train and to further the development of, as in "foster". Very similar to those who foster children, "to foster" means to give care to and to promote the growth; development and encouragement. In the New Testament the word nurture in the Greek is "paideia" (pahee-di'-ah); tutorage, i.e. education or training; and implies disciplinary correction: chastening, chastisement, instruction.[xxxi] When we think of nurturing we do not think of growing; we would rather stay as babies to receive constant affection and other things that babies get. We do not think of education because we have all of the answers and we certainly do not think of discipline because we will think we are being abused. Surely this is not what a nurturing pastor signs up for! One of the worst things that a pastor can experience is when a needy person is waiting daily for a deposit of constant affirmation and attention from them. It can add to an already heavy load, things that are not necessary which can become tiresome and unhealthy

So then who determines whether or not nurturing is needed or has taken place? The Lord is the one who knows our every need. He knows what we need and if—in fact—we need the nurturing we so desire.

There are so many places in scripture where we see nurturing, teaching, training and grooming. Jesus had a name for the groups of people that he nurtured. They were called disciples. The word disciple means one who accepts and assists in spreading the doctrines of another, a convinced adherent of a school or individual. [xxxii] In general, apostles refer to a small, inner group of Jesus' followers; disciples refer to a larger group of Jesus' followers. We are all, in many ways, students and disciples of Jesus Christ, which means we are all being nurtured by Him in some way, form or fashion.

The Responsibility of Those Being Nurtured

What are the responsibilities for those of us who are being nurtured by Him? We as disciples of Jesus

Christ have a responsibility to study to show ourselves approved unto God (II Tim. 2:15). This means that it is important to know the teachings of Jesus! We cannot be lazy disciples; we must put in time to learn. If we are being nurtured or trained in the way of the Scriptures, it does not matter who trains us. How much of a good student we become is what matters. A good student will be diligent in studying. We are ultimately disciples of Jesus before anyone else, so His teachings are paramount.

Sometimes we look at the vessels that God has chosen to train us and when they are not effective in teaching us what we need to know, we fall short in our training, forgetting that we have to ultimately give an account to God. When I was in grade school, I had a math teacher whose assignment was to teach me multiplication and division. He wasn't really reaching me with his style of teaching and as a result I fell back in the subject. Not doing well at that time crippled me in Math and eventually in other areas of my life. I couldn't do algebra because I was not proficient in the basics of math. I could very well blame my teacher, but there is no excuse. I could also blame my parents, but coming from a dysfunctional home, I guess I was fortunate enough to even be in class, much less getting someone to help me with my studies. Later on in life, I had the opportunity to hone in on my mathematical challenges, but they were not as important to me as some other things were. Can I learn math? Yes I can. Can I take one of the many courses and find creative ways to do so? Yes I can. I do have choices in life. I choose to learn! All students have choices. Even those who have learning disabilities have opportunities afforded to them to be able to better themselves.

So what is the point? Students have responsibilities to their teachers, to God and themselves! And as pastors, we need to find ourselves in study so that we will have something to offer those we are accountable for. Let us not find ourselves falling short in the area of study and placing blame on others. Get excited about the ability to learn and the many ways in which we can do so.

The Responsibility to Supply Nourishment

God has given his ministers and pastors a mandate to feed His sheep. Today that mandate still stands! God is looking for those who will still feed His sheep and young lambs. Too many of our leaders are falling short in this area. We are not putting in proper study time so that the food for God's people is sufficient for sustenance. We have allowed conferences and television ministries to be the sole place for feeding God's people His word. Today's spiritual food is no longer found by going to Sunday morning service at the local church. People have formed Sunday morning rituals of obtaining spiritual food through the various media outlets (e.g. TV, internet, radio). And the preaching that is offered through these outlets is so watered down; it is a wonder that the people of God have the ability to withstand the wiles of the enemy today.

The seriousness of all of this is that we have to give an account to God for our responsibility to His sheep. The average Christian and new convert are so undernourished today and we are leaving them helpless to the dangers around them. Many Pastors are collecting large salaries and are not even putting the time into successfully feeding the sheep.

Sometimes feeding the sheep can get a little mundane, especially when you have been doing it the same way for so many years. This may mean giving yourself to prayer and asking God for creative ways to do continual feeding. Fresh ideas are always good, although, traditional situations still work. In addition to the usual Sunday morning feeding, you can find creative ways of getting the Scriptures into your growing and eager people. Be open to new ideas and be alert for others that the Lord may want to use. Sometimes doing all the work can make one resentful about doing the feeding.

Training and Educating

I was reared in a church that has often been called a training center. When ministers or even congregants relocated into other areas, the leaders of the other congregations were often so impressed by the amount of word our people knew and lived. I am still thankful today for that training and *the words* that those leaders shared (Many are still training today). However, there will always be people who will be sitting under such training "looking for training". Please do not measure your training on their understanding of whether or not they are receiving training. Miserable, rebellious and or fickle people may never see the things they should.

I am presently attending a church that loves nurturing and grooming. I, too, am a recipient and a part of that process. My present pastor finds so many creative ways in which to train her leaders. One way that I thought was very creative was taking a couple of us to classes which she herself had to attend for seminary. She did the bulk of her course study on line, and over the course of the two year period of study, she was required to take several trips to certain campuses for additional study and seminars. She received full credit for each seminar and because continuing education hours were given for those classes and seminars as well, I went along with her and attended her classes as well. This was another level of training for me. Because of the variety of the courses/seminars, it only added to the creativity of the training and education process for her budding trainees. The information that I received was priceless and will always remain with me. It has certainly prepared me for any additional formal training that I would receive further up the road.

Seminars and mini courses can make for a wonderful training experience. Unless you don't have a specific expertise in a particular area, you should feel free to do your own training. If there are others in your midsts that have this ability, you can put them in place. Ultimately, everything or every person that you need could very well already be "in house". If you are a pastor whom the Lord has called and you are in the situation where the Lord has placed you, then you can count on His provision in this area. Sending people out to seminars that you hear of can add to your pool of training. For instance, there are so many praise and worship seminars throughout the country. A faithful worship leader that can attend the training would bring back information and begin to train others around them. If you have a few faithful worship leaders, you may want to send three or four of them. They can come back and share the load. I would recommend that if you pay for a portion of or all of the training, you require that they commit to a certain amount of years of service. Many people who are sent for training often get weird revelations and decide to take that training and use it in another vineyard.

Sometimes bringing in outsiders can add to the variety and make training a great deal easier; however, you do not want to make this your norm. It can make those whom you are training dependent on the voice of outsiders for validation of good training. The Bible is a good training manual, and it has everything needed for ministry. It may mean broadening your scope and studying areas with which you are not yet familiar. The study can do you a world of good as it will keep you on the cutting edge with fresh new ideas regularly. It will require work on your part, so if you are a lazy leader, work on the discipline of study.

Other ways of nurturing can include regular lunch and breakfast sessions. These can be times when you share ideas with your people and they can hear your heart. Share your burden and keep your vision before them; this can be done individually or in small groups. It also gives your potential leaders an opportunity to fellowship and report to you their progress and any complaints or troubles they may be facing.

Grooming and Pouring Into Leaders

Grooming takes getting up close and personal with potential leaders. It may mean anything from talking about hygiene to deportment and handling personal business. Of course it forces you to step up in those areas as well because you have to "practice what you preach", but that's par for the course.

This means if you find that they have bad body odor, you tell them so with love. If you see where they are going astray in different areas, sometimes even if you are not sure, you need to speak up and confront them. If you get wind of sloppy business procedures, expose them. This is what makes a person know that you care. Many people do not have the courage to help people personally, but to those of us who do, know that you do a world of good in doing so.

I can recall a few years back when my former Pastor (and sister) took me aside and told me that I had an odor. While I knew that she was accurate, I denied it. I knew that I was not consistent in the area of hygiene, because washing up didn't come naturally to me. So I walked around smelly most of the time. Initially when she told me, I got angry at all those whom she represented. After all she did tell me that she was not the only one who smelled me. Why couldn't the others come to me? Why didn't they have the courage to tell me? Didn't they love me enough to not have me stinking up the place? What I've come to learn is that not everyone thinks loving confrontation is easy. As a matter of fact, many people find it very hard to do. A good leader who loves their people will lovingly cover them by letting them know their faults even when those who are being confronted don't see it in themselves. Be patient. When one is confronted, he or she may initially deny it out of embarrassment, but hang in there for you will soon see the fruit of your labor.

There were so many times when my present pastor would help me to understand the logistics of how to put together something as basic as clothing. She taught me when teaching, business suits were appropriate; when preaching, we should wear something that didn't call attention to ourselves and when ministering not to subscribe to a great deal of loud colors. She taught me how to look appropriate in the supermarket just in case you are noticed by one of the members or anyone else that would respect your call.

These are the kinds of things that are not generally placed in books, but God is interested in the whole person. I am so glad He saw fit to polish me up with those that "braved the storm". I wasn't an easy pupil! Parenting is crucial to a person's deportment. My parents died when I was young and tender, so a great deal of grooming never took place.

I thank God that He had nurturing in the plan for grooming me.

Character and Deportment

A cousin of mine once shared with me, early in ministry, about carriage and deportment. While she didn't give a great deal of tips she told me about two musician friends of mine. One was gifted but carried herself in a manner that wasn't positive. She dressed weird, was eccentric in her attitude and very dull in her senses. The other was equally gifted but was always found dressed impeccably well, sharp in her senses and because she was consistently working on her spiritual life, she was sober minded. While one could have had more gifting then the other, it was assumed that the one that was impeccably dressed was considered a much better musician. That didn't have to be so, but her carriage and deportment took her where her gift could not. Sometimes this necessary ingredient can make the difference as to whether or not someone is received in their gifting and calling.

Many of us can nurture others with the nurturing that we have received, but we are neglectful because we feel we won't be received.

I believe that if God sends you people to groom you need to do just that remembering we ultimately have to give an account to God for those we have ignored.

Lastly it is so important to encourage potential leaders. It can mean pushing them into place and into situations that they otherwise would not go. Perhaps they feel inadequate, but push them to grow and do things on their own. Again, many people did not receive this from their parenting and it is necessary to the growth of an individual. You will be surprised at how many can blossom with regular encouragement and affirmation from their leader.

A great deal of leaders lack in this area because they feel that it may do more harm than good, not to mention the fact that we, too, are insecure and don't want others to feel better than we feel about ourselves. This means there is some serious healing that needs to take place in the Pastors as well. If this is left neglected, it could mean the people will look to get grooming and affirmation elsewhere, especially in places where they should not. If an outside leader begins nurturing your leaders, there is a possibility that you may lose your potential leaders to those who are nurturing them. This means your healing is urgent and very necessary so that others can benefit from it.

Anything that is planted needs nurturing and all Christians need nurturing in order to grow. Pastors should find themselves nurturing their leaders and their leaders in turn should nurture the congregants. If this is done, I believe that we would have less people leaving churches. Many people leave their churches because they feel that they are getting nurturing somewhere else, or they feel that they can get nurturing somewhere else. Leaders and people that are nurtured in a healthy way will turn around and nurture others and make for a healthy environment. Do not let your lack in this area send your sheep running out the door.

If you do your part, somebody else will do theirs, and God will give the increase! **1Cor. 3:7**
So let's get started nurturing God's leaders. Below are some practical ideas that may prove helpful.

Getting Started

Schedule designated time to brainstorm. Sometimes Saturday morning meetings with coffee and danishes can turn something that would appear mundane into something more interesting.

1. Always follow up and follow through on everything that you begin. This will make each potential leader know that you are serious about what you have put in place. If you are not sure that you can follow through, designate a person that will do so for you. This will assure that you keep your word to them so they do not become "weary in well doing", at least not from this particular situation.

2. Develop stronger study time for yourself, so that you will consistently have a well of resources within yourself. This may mean going out to different seminars as well. Always seek to better yourself.

3. It is very easy to groom the ones that want grooming, but it is not always so easy to groom the ones that do not want it, even though the Lord has given you the mandate to do so. Grooming the ones that may not be as open will keep you on your knees in prayer! Prayer is necessary for grooming others; especially difficult ones. Start with prayer and then by loving them. It may take some time, but God will accomplish this work through you as you yield yourself to Him (1 Cor. 12:31).

The Conclusion of the Matter

Today Grace Temple Church is a thriving church. It survived its devastation by the will of the Lord, and the obedience of Alma Seymour the late pastor's wife. She remembers conversations and concerns Pastor Seymour had regarding some of the potential leaders in the church and some of the commendations as well. With this knowledge and with the help and counsel of many of those in her path, Grace Temple was still afloat after what seemed to be year of labor, toil and much prayer and the help of the Holy Spirit.

Alma Seymour was able to successfully identify those that are now helping to continue the legacy that Pastor Seymour left behind. Ordination day was fast approaching and she had several candidates being groomed and nurtured.

Those individuals that joined the ministry that were already ordained ministers were preparing to officially transfer their credentials with equal training and development procedures. Things were looking up, members were hopeful and it was evident that God was in the midst.

In conclusion, always know that God will not leave Himself without a witness. He is not sloppy, inconsistent or negligent, even when we ourselves are. In His will, there is safety and provision. Look for it! When it looks like you have been abandoned or overlooked, take a second look and see the great wealth of his work.

Chapter Reflections

To Potential Leaders:

1. Do you believe you need nurturing? Do you see where God has already nurtured you in some way?
2. Do others in authority notice your "fruit" or is it hidden, dormant or useless?
3. Is there anything that stops you from trusting the leader that God has placed you under? If so (in your opinion), is it something in you or something in the leader?
4. If you are certain that God has placed you in your church, are you willing to trust that, move ahead and follow His plan for you in that church despite your feelings?
5. Do you find yourself discussing and rehearsing the negative issues with someone else in the congregation or are you using the biblical method to handle issues? What is usually the outcome?

Plan of Action:

Begin by acknowledging and accepting the Sovereignty of God. Seek Him for direction regarding the leader and ministry He would have you to commit to.

Once you are certain, Trust His perfect leading and trust the people that were put in place to shepherd your soul; though imperfect, you have to believe that they are God's choice for you. Lastly, give every talent and gift back to The Lord. Allow Him to use it for the Kingdom and fruit will be yielded for His glory.

To Pastors:

Are there any skilled people in the congregation that you have considered grooming for leadership in some area of the church? If so ask yourself the following questions:

1. Is this person stable in their emotions?
2. Do they have their own plans in addition to God's plan?

3. Do you have a relationship with this person to answer these questions?
4. Do they hold onto the word? Are they doers of the word?
5. Do they have tendencies to "abandon ship"?
6. Do you see the fruit of the spirit at work in the person's life?
7. Are there any young persons who show evidence of a relationship with the Lord, if so, how closely connected are you to the young people in your church?

Plan of Action:

Discernment is necessary to the task at hand. If you lack discernment, focus on maturing in the area of your own spiritual growth (seeing that this is necessary to discernment). Pray, and ask the Lord to help you discern whether a person is carnal or Spiritual. God may choose to send you a carnal person to work with. If so, accept that it will require work on your part as well. This includes prayer, patience, consistent exhorting and confrontation.

Endnotes

---

[i] Adam Clarke's Commentary, Electronic Database. Copyright (c) 1996 by Biblesoft

[ii] http://www.christianitytoday.com/le/thepastor/pastorsrole/goodnewsbadnews.html

[iii] ibid

[iv] ibid

[v] Damazio, Frank, "The Making of a Leader", Copyright © 1988, City Bible Publishing, Inc. Portland, OR 1988

[vi] Adam Clarke's Commentary, Electronic Database. Copyright © 1996, 2003 by Biblesoft, Inc.

[vii] ibid

[viii] Adam Clarke's Commentary, Electronic Database. Copyright (c) 1996 by Biblesoft

[ix] Adam Clarke's Commentary, Electronic Database. Copyright (c) 1996 by Biblesoft

[x] ibid

[xi] Matthew Henry's Commentary on the Whole Bible: New Modern Edition, Electronic Database. Copyright (c) 1991 by Hendrickson Publishers, Inc.

[xii] Adam Clarke's Commentary, Electronic Database. Copyright (c) 1996 by Biblesoft

[xiii] Ibid.

[xiv] High Maintenance Relationships, Copyright ©1996 , Tyndale House Publishers

[xv] Biblesoft's New Exhaustive Strong's Numbers and Concordance with Expanded Greek-Hebrew Dictionary. Copyright © 1994, 2003 Biblesoft, Inc. and International Bible Translators, Inc.

[xvi] Vine's Expository Dictionary of Biblical Words, Copyright © 1985, Thomas Nelson Publishers.

[xvii] Biblesoft's New Exhaustive Strong's Numbers and Concordance with Expanded Greek-Hebrew Dictionary. Copyright © 1994, 2003 Biblesoft, Inc. and International

Bible Translators, Inc.
[xviii] Adam Clarke's Commentary, Electronic Database. Copyright © 1996, 2003 by Biblesoft, Inc. All rights reserved.
[xix] ibid
[xx] ibid
[xxi] Adam Clarke's Commentary, Electronic Database. Copyright © 1996, 2003 by Biblesoft, Inc. All rights reserved.
[xxii] ibid
[xxiii] ibid
[xxiv] Adam Clarke's Commentary, Electronic Database. Copyright (c) 1996 by Biblesoft
[xxv] Biblesoft's New Exhaustive Strong's Numbers and Concordance with Expanded Greek-Hebrew Dictionary. Copyright (c) 1994
[xxvi] Mclintock and Strong Encyclopedia, Electronic Database. Copyright (c) 2000 by Biblesoft
[xxvii] McClintock and Strong Encyclopedia, Electronic Database. Copyright (c) 2000 by Biblesoft
[xxviii] Barnes' Notes, Electronic Database. Copyright (c) 1997 by Biblesoft
[xxix]http://encarta.msn.com/encnet/features/dictionary/DictionaryResults.aspx?refid=1861673846
[xxx]International Standard Bible Encyclopaedia, Electronic Database Copyright (c)1996 by Biblesoft
[xxxi] Biblesoft's New Exhaustive Strong's Numbers and Concordance with Expanded Greek-Hebrew Dictionary. Copyright © 1994, 2003 Biblesoft, Inc. and International Bible Translators, Inc.
[xxxii]Nelson's Illustrated Bible Dictionary

Bibliography

http://www.christianitytoday.com/le/thepastor/pastorsrole/goodnewsbadnews.html

Adam Clarke's Commentary, Electronic Database. Copyright (c) 1996 by Biblesoft

Barnes' Notes, Electronic Database. Copyright (c) 1997 by Biblesoft

Biblesoft's New Exhaustive Strong's Numbers and Concordance with Expanded Greek-Hebrew Dictionary. Copyright © 1994, 2003 Biblesoft, Inc. and International Bible Translators, Inc.

Damazio, Frank, "The Making of a Leader", Copyright © 1988, City Bible Publishing, Inc. Portland, OR 1988

High Maintenance Relationships, Copyright ©1996 , Tyndale House Publishers

International Standard Bible Encyclopaedia, Electronic Database Copyright (c)1996 by Biblesoft

Matthew Henry's Commentary on the Whole Bible: New Modern Edition, Electronic Database. Copyright (c) 1991 by Hendrickson Publishers, Inc.

Mclintock and Strong Encyclopedia, Electronic Database. Copyright (c) 2000 by Biblesoft

Nelson's Illustrated Bible Dictionary

Vine's Expository Dictionary of Biblical Words, Copyright © 1985, Thomas Nelson Publishers

Contact Us

The International Gathering at
Beth Rapha
1540 Route 202 Suite 3
Pomona, NY 10970
845. 369.8900

Precious JEM Ministries, Inc
P.O. Box 684
Pomona, NY 10970

Bright Light Publishers, Inc
P.O. Box 684
Pomona, NY 10970

Made in the USA
Middletown, DE
07 November 2019

78035603R00109